THE REVENGE OF HISTORY

THE REVENGE OF HISTORY

MARXISM AND THE EAST EUROPEAN REVOLUTIONS

Alex Callinicos

The Pennsylvania State University Press
University Park, Pennsylvania

Copyright © A. T. Callinicos 1991

First published 1991 in the United States by
The Pennsylvania State University Press,
Suite C, 820 North University Drive,
University Park, PA 16802

ISBN 0–271–00767–2 (cloth)
ISBN 0–271–00768–0 (paper)

Library of Congress Cataloging in Publication Data
A CIP catalogue record for this book is available from
the Library of Congress

It is the policy of The Pennsylvania State University Press to use acid-free paper
for the first printing of all clothbound books. Publications on uncoated stock
satisfy minimum requirements of American National Standard for Information
Sciences — Permanence of Paper for Printed Library Materials,
ANSI 239.48-1984

Typeset in 10½ on 12 pt Sabon
by Wearside Tradespools, Fulwell, Sunderland
Printed in Great Britain by T.J. Press, Padstow, Cornwall

'The vengeance of history is more powerful than the vengeance of the most powerful General Secretary.'

Leon Trotsky

'Die Weltgeschichte is das Weltgericht.' ('World history is the world's judgement.')

Friedrich von Schiller

To Tony Cliff, the pilot who weathered the storm

CONTENTS

PREFACE AND ACKNOWLEDGEMENTS

One of my greatest sources of pleasure and inspiration in the past few years has been the opportunities there have increasingly been to meet socialists – real socialists, that is, not Stalinist apologists – from what we must now stop calling the Eastern bloc. These meetings have been one reason among many for refusing to believe in the widely announced death of socialism. To hear, for example, Boris Kagarlitsky in September 1989, on the eve of the East European revolutions, deliver his Isaac Deutscher Memorial Lecture in London to an audience including, alongside hundreds of enthusiastic young socialists, the South African metalworkers' leader Moses Mayekiso was to have a sense of an international socialist movement re-emerging sixty years after it was destroyed by Stalin and Hitler. This book is, among other things, a contribution to what should be an international dialogue on the left about the implications of the collapse of Stalinism for the theory and practice of socialism.

I bring to this discussion no great specialist knowledge of the USSR and Eastern Europe. Things Russian have nevertheless loomed quite large in my life one way and another, and I have incurred many debts. I would like therefore to greet my old cronies Olga Semonova and Victor Haynes, and to thank Xan and Jane Smiley, whose kindness to me during my stay with them in Moscow went well beyond the requirements of hospitality or kinship. David Held has been, once again, all that one could ask of an editor, nobly ignoring the criticisms I make of some of his views in this book.

All of the above would, I imagine, wish to disclaim any responsibility for what follows. There are others, however, who cannot get off so lightly. Tony Cliff formulated over forty years ago the theory of state capitalism on which I draw so heavily in this book; the revolutions of

1989 have vindicated his life-work and it is only appropriate therefore that I should dedicate this book to him. Chris Harman has
provided over the past two decades a quite unmatched analysis of the
crisis of the Stalinist regimes. My debt to both is immeasurable. They
read this book in draft, as did John Rees, who also suggested its title. I
am grateful to all three for their help. Rarely have I been more aware
of how comparatively limited the contribution of the individual
author is, though naturally only I can be held to account for the final
result.

INTRODUCTION

Any lengthy attempt to explain why I have written this book would be beside the point. The revolutions which transformed Eastern Europe in the last three months of 1989 were that rare thing, genuinely world-shaking events. Efforts to capture their scale have long since passed into platitude. But the political earthquake in the East represents more than the collapse of six regimes* or the consequent reorganization of the international state-system. It is an ideological event of the first magnitude. The official religion of the Russian empire was Marxism-Leninism. One factor in the hollowing out of this ideology which long preceded the fall of the regimes it sought to legitimize was the stagnation induced by the bureaucratic command economies of the Eastern bloc. And so the disintegration of Communist party rule has been proclaimed to augur the death of Marxism, indeed of socialism itself.

The aim of this book is simple enough – to block this inference, to deny that the death agony of Stalinism amounts to the bankruptcy of the revolutionary socialist tradition founded by Marx. My intention here is not to anticipate the arguments which are developed in the chapters that follow. But it is worth highlighting one point. This book is a defence of Marxism. It is, however, undertaken from a perspective which most Marxist intellectuals would probably regard as eccentric. Marxism enjoyed, as a result of the great commotions of the late 1960s and early 1970s, an enormous intellectual revival whose effects are still felt in the academy, especially in the English-speaking world, despite the many disappointments and defeats suffered by the Western left in the 1980s. But valuable, sometimes brilliant, though much of the output of this academic Marxism has

*Poland, Hungary, East Germany, Bulgaria, Czechoslovakia, Romania.

been, it has, as I try to show below, found great difficulty in making sense of the crisis in the Eastern bloc.

The reason is, I think, political. Left-wing intellectuals have tended to assume that there are only two socialist traditions of any moment. The first is what is sometimes called orthodox Communism or Marxism-Leninism, but which I prefer to call Stalinism – until recently the state ideology in the East, which identifies socialism with one-party rule and bureaucratic command economy. In its Russian version this brand of socialism long ago lost its political sex appeal in the West (although the Third World has been a different matter). In the 1960s and 1970s, however, many Western Marxists were attracted to the 'left' variant of Stalinism that traded under the name of Maoism. When *that* God failed, the only alternative (for those who wanted to remain socialists) was the other main tradition of the left, social democracy, which seeks to transform, or at least to ameliorate, capitalism within the framework of Western liberal democracy. Those with justifiable qualms caused by the unsavoury record of social democrats in office – the policies of Mitterrand, González, Papandreou, Hawke, and Lange in the 1980s differed little from those of Reagan, Kohl, and Thatcher – might look towards the Greens, but their performance suggested that they were more likely to amount to little more than a tributary of, rather than an alternative to, the parties of the Second International.

Now the main assumption of this book is that the choice facing socialists is not exhausted by these unappetizing alternatives of Stalinism and social democracy. There is a third great socialist tradition, the revolutionary one founded by Marx and Engels and continued principally by Lenin and the Bolsheviks, by Trotsky and the Left Opposition, by Luxemburg and by Gramsci. Thus insisting on the specificity of the revolutionary socialist tradition, of what Isaac Deutscher called classical Marxism, involves denying what is treated as axiomatic by every mainstream commentator and most socialists, namely that Stalin continued and indeed consummated the revolution led by Lenin in October 1917 and therefore that it is 'Leninism' that has collapsed in the East. And that is precisely what I do deny: Stalinism represented a counter-revolution, the final liquidation of everything the October Revolution had sought to achieve. If this – I believe, historically demonstrable – claim is true, then the meaning of the East European revolutions is very different from that normally given them. What is dying in the disintegrating Eastern bloc is not socialism, of however a degenerate and distorted form, but the negation of socialism. Its collapse may thus allow the authentic

Marxist tradition, long driven underground, to return to the light of day.

It is one thing to say this, quite another to provide convincing arguments in its support. I offer what I hope are such arguments in what follows. I do not claim, however, to provide here a general defence of Marxism against *all* significant criticism. My focus is on the issues raised by the death agony of Stalinism, and my choice of topics reflects this: even my treatment of the history of the USSR and Eastern Europe is highly selective, and I ignore entirely Stalinist regimes in the Third World such as China and Cuba. I have discussed other important questions elsewhere, notably in two other books which, in retrospect rather than in conception, form a trilogy with this one: *Making History* (1987) offers a philosophical elaboration of the Marxist theory of history and revolution, while *Against Postmodernism* (1990) attacks the idea that we live in a qualitatively new, 'postindustrial' epoch. I largely take for granted here the arguments of these books, though acquaintance with them is in no sense a precondition for appreciating what follows. The fact that another issue – that of gender – is not considered here does not mean that I have any doubts about its importance: it has, however, been dealt with very well by Lindsey German in *Sex, Class and Socialism* (1989).

Governed by these constraints, the book's shape is simple enough. Chapter 1 reflects on the experience of 1989, records its dominant interpretation, on the left as well as the right, as the end of Marxism, and seeks to clarify what I understand by the revolutionary socialist tradition. Chapter 2 analyses that tradition's greatest triumph and failure, the October Revolution, tracing the development of Stalinism from the early days of soviet power to the era of *perestroika*, and exploring the nature and limits of the crisis now breaking up that economic and political system. In chapter 3 I seek to deflate the triumphalism which proclaims this crisis as the victory of liberal capitalism, examining the conflicts among the Western powers which the convulsions in the East are likely if anything to exacerbate. Finally, in chapter 4 I try to vindicate the classical Marxist vision of socialism as an order superior to really existing capitalism in both its main current versions – the bureaucratic state capitalism of the East and the regulated market economies of the West. I hope thus to have provided firm grounding for my conclusion – that the East European revolutions should be seen not primarily as a crisis for the left, but as an opportunity finally to free socialism from the incubus of Stalinism.

1

THE END OF SOCIALISM?

'Revolution is the inspired frenzy of history.'

Leon Trotsky

1.1 THE INSPIRED FRENZY OF HISTORY

It still seems extraordinary that 1989 should have turned out to be a year of revolution. For the mood in the West was profoundly conservative. Still basking in the economic recovery that had prevailed throughout much of the decade, the advanced capitalist countries represented that portion of the globe from which the idea of revolution had long since apparently been banished. The fact that 1989 marked the bicentenary of the Great French Revolution served only to underline this fact. Best seller on both sides of the Atlantic was Simon Schama's *Citizens*, a book which, reflecting the anti-Marxist consensus now prevailing among historians of the Revolution, offered a modish repackaging of the conservative view of 1789 and its aftermath: like his forebears from Burke onwards, Schama painted a portrait of the Revolution as a demonic outburst of irrational violence, but tricked it out with all the considerable rhetorical devices at his command, with the latest historiographic techniques, and with obeisances to feminism, so that, for example, the Great Fear figured mainly as an unpleasant interruption of the Marquise de La Tour du Pin's holidays. The commercial message was plain enough: revolutions were a Bad Thing, bloody, destructive, irrational.

Even the French Prime Minister, Michel Rocard, justified the lavish commemoration of 1789 by his government on the grounds that 'it convinced a lot of people that revolution is dangerous and that if one can do without it, so much the better'.[1] The broad currents of informed opinion in the West shared this attitude. Daniel Bell's announcement of 'The End of Ideology' had apparently been proved true, thirty years after it had been made in the late 1950s. For the white-collar 'new middle class' who had done so well out of economic growth in the 1980s, the good life seemed to consist in following the cues offered by the knowing lower-case yuppie social comedies so popular at the end of the decade, *thirtysomething* and *sex, lies and videotape*, and cultivating the pleasures and anxieties of personal relationships. Should anyone require intellectual reassurance about following this course, 'postmodernist' philosophers such as Richard Rorty were on hand to argue that the 'grand narratives' of human emancipation constructed by Hegel and Marx were all bunk and to celebrate the emergence in the West of an 'increasingly ironist culture' dominated by 'the pursuit of private perfection'.[2]

It is hard to imagine a political and cultural climate less well equipped to make sense of what actually happened in 1989. First the students of China rose up, taking to the streets to demand democratic rights, and, for a while, humiliating the country's geriatric rulers. When the army was mobilized to crush the student demonstrators in Tiananmen Square, it found the working-class neighbourhoods of Beijing blocked against it, as the entire population of this and other Chinese cities rallied behind the democracy movement. Even the terrible massacre of 3–4 June, when what was becoming a rising by both students and workers against the Communist Party regime was drowned in blood, left behind it one indelible image of courage and defiance, when the whole world saw a lone youth halt a column of tanks.[3]

Tiananmen in one sense was poor preparation for what followed in Eastern Europe. It reinforced the picture of 'really existing socialism' as a monolith profoundly resistant to real change. Fear of instability had led China's rulers to rein back the economic reforms they had earlier introduced and to destroy the democracy movement. But the reform process initiated in the USSR after Mikhail Gorbachev's installation as General Secretary of the Communist Party of the Soviet Union in March 1985 had very different and quite unexpected results in Eastern Europe.[4] It permitted the Polish and Hungarian regimes to seek to overcome their own crises of growth and of legitimacy by concluding, in the spring of 1989, round-table agreements with the opposition, agreements whose most spectacular outcome was the victory of Solidarność in the elections of 4 June, and the formation, two and a half months later, of a coalition government of the former antagonists, the union and the (soon to disband) Communist Party. It was a by-product of these changes, however, which unleashed the decisive process of transformation in Eastern Europe. Hungary's opening of its border with Austria permitted what soon became a massive emigration of East Germans to the West. The East German regime had the carpet pulled from under it when Gorbachev, visiting East Berlin on 7 October, made it clear that Moscow would not sanction the use of force to crush the mass demonstrations which the emigration and changes elsewhere in the Eastern bloc stimulated in Leipzig and other cities. Its solution, to reassure the populace by opening the Berlin Wall on 9 November, marked instead not simply the collapse of Communist Party rule but – beyond all realistic hopes and fears – the imminent reunification of Germany.

The German events soon found echoes in Czechoslovakia. As in China, students started the earthquake, but with happier results. The brutal suppression of a student demonstration in Prague on 17 November evoked a massive response. Czechoslovakia's rulers, installed in power when Russian tanks crushed the Prague Spring in August 1968, were hoist by their own petard, denied the option of a Tiananmen-style massacre by Soviet opposition to repression. On 24 November Alexander Dubček was given a hero's welcome in Wenceslas Square and the Communist Party leadership resigned. By the end of the year the opposition playwright Václav Havel had been installed as President, and Czechoslovakia, along with the rest of Eastern Europe, was on the road to liberal democracy. But by then the most extraordinary change of all had happened. The one regime to attempt to repeat Deng Xiaoping's success in crushing popular resistance, the demented Stalinist despotism of Nicolae Ceauşescu in Romania, was overthrown by armed insurrection. For the first time since the far-off days of Franco's triumph over the Republicans in Spain, Europe echoed to the sounds of civil war. Barely had the world had a chance to absorb the impact of the Christmas Revolution, when the USSR itself seemed to enter a new and darker phase of the era of *glasnost* and *perestroika*, as Gorbachev concentrated vast powers in his hands as executive President and moved to confront the nationalist movements threatening the integrity of the Soviet Union in Transcaucasia and the Baltic. The chapter of astonishing changes which had begun what seemed a lifetime ago, in the spring of 1989, did not seem yet to have closed.

But what did the revolutions that had already happened mean? The peoples of Eastern Europe made it plain what the changes meant for *them*, through their own action and especially in the extraordinary scenes of public happiness that formed so powerful and moving a part of the revolutions. But matters were different for people in the West, who could only participate in these events vicariously: not the least remarkable thing about 1989 was the way in which global communications allowed vast television audiences around the world to eavesdrop on great happenings, on scenes of horror – the tanks rumbling into Tiananmen Square – and of great joy – the cheering crowds surging through the Berlin Wall. Almost everyone welcomed the changes. It was indeed amusing to observe Western commentators, who not long before had been damning revolution as the greatest of political sins, briskly excuse the hasty disposal of the Ceauşescus, invoking the same remorseless political logic used to justify the executions of Louis XVI of France and Nicholas II of Russia. Hugh Trevor-Roper, the doyen of conservative historians, cheerfully dismissed the affair thus:

> No doubt a formal trial would have looked better. But in revolutions events move fast and men must act. Dictators who have so visibly brought their countries to ruin and have openly claimed responsibility for their crimes have forfeited their civil rights. They are as pirates, 'enemies of the human race', and it is as well they should know it. Historians can catch up afterwards.[5]

But the Western establishment's new-found tolerance of revolutionary violence was of less significance than other considerations. Many in the advanced capitalist world must have felt the contrast between their own situation and the events appearing on their television screens. The joy displayed by East European demonstrators seemed to involve more than a reaction to the fall of hated regimes or the (probably unrealistic) anticipation of the delights of the consumer society. It appeared to represent the felt recovery of collective agency. These were peoples raised up morally by the sense that they could gain some control over the world, could remake the societies in which they lived. Yet the condition of Western liberal democracies – supposedly the goal of the revolutions of 1989 – was notoriously one in which the public sphere had been corroded, in which social experience was profoundly fragmented, in which citizens' private lives had become the main centre of their emotional and material investments, their chief source of pleasure and fulfilment. The resulting contrast was perhaps strongest during the Romanian Revolution of December 1989. Amidst the consumerist daze that is a modern Christmas, Western television viewers could follow a revolutionary drama that strictly observed the patterns laid down in 1789, 1848, and 1917. No wonder that 1989 left George Steiner gloomily wondering whether '[t]he knout on the one hand; the cheeseburger on the other' exhausted the alternatives facing human civilization.[6]

For all that, the strongest feeling created by the revolutions of 1989 was one of exhilaration. Far beyond the countries directly affected, people shared a sense of suddenly widened possibilities. Parts of the furniture of the postwar world that had seemed irremovable suddenly disappeared – literally in the case of the Berlin Wall. Previously unalterable assumptions – for example, that Europe would be permanently divided between the superpowers – abruptly collapsed. It seemed as if the world had suddenly woken up from a long sleep. This feeling was strongest in Europe, the continent most directly affected, but it found its echoes elsewhere – in the Middle East for example, and in South Africa, where a process of authoritarian reform analogous to Gorbachev's led in February 1990 to the long-awaited release of Nelson Mandela. It seemed as if the world might be made anew.

1.2   FAREWELL TO MARX?

How strange, then, that the most celebrated interpretation of the collapse of Stalinism should predict the world's entry into 'centuries of boredom' brought about by the 'unabashed victory of economic and political liberalism', marking not merely the 'triumph of the West', but 'the end of history as such: that is, the end point of mankind's ideological evolution and the universalization of Western liberal democracy as the final form of human government'. Francis Fukuyama's instantly famous essay actually preceded the East European revolutions, appearing in the summer of 1989. Nevertheless, its pertinence was, if anything, reinforced by the upheavals of the months following its publication. Fukuyama's numerous critics were quick to identify many of the essay's chief faults. Most obviously, its theoretical framework was provided by Alexandre Kojève's interpretation of Hegel's philosophy of history. Kojève's lectures on Hegel had an important impact on the Parisian intellectual scene in the 1930s; his reappearance in America fifty years later, first as a character in Saul Bellow's novel *More Die of Heartbreak*, then as a major influence on the Deputy Director of the Policy Planning Staff at the State Department, is one of the more bizarre episodes in recent cultural history. Fukuyama extracted two main claims from Hegel and Kojève: first, that conflicts between ideologies constitute the motor of history, and secondly, that liberalism is the last major ideology. From these two premises he drew the conclusion that history is over. But even if both propositions accurately capture Hegel's thought (which is doubtful), there is no particular reason to believe either of them: Fukuyama's attempts to explain away the persistence of nationalism and revival of religious fundamentalism as 'impulses incompletely played out, even in parts of the post-historical world' were especially unconvincing. The apologetic element in the essay was all too evident, as in the almost engagingly absurd claim that 'the egalitarianism of modern America represents the essential achievement of the classless society envisioned by Marx' – inner cities hollowed out by warring drug gangs were of course very much part of Marx's scheme for communism.⁷ One could see why Fukuyama's essay was the toast of Washington, offering as it did a reassuring counterpoint to Paul Kennedy's equally celebrated prediction in *The Rise and Fall of the Great Powers* that the United States must follow Spain and Britain into imperial decline as its economic supremacy is eroded by rivals such as Japan. 'No wonder "Endism" has gone down so well', Paul Hirst comments: 'it has provided a sophisticated rationale for the commonplaces of American political life.'⁸

The fact remains, however, that for all the eccentricity of Fukuyama's philosophical views and the signs of his essay's origins in the Bush administration, he expressed the spirit of the time. Most of his critics conceded, in Edward Mortimer's words, that Fukuyama's 'main point – the current lack of competitors against political and economic liberalism in the world ideological market place – is surely hard to refute'.⁹ Even the idea of the end of history struck a chord. Fukuyama concluded his essay by saying:

> The end of history will be a very sad time. The struggle for recognition, the willingness to risk one's life for a purely abstract goal, the worldwide ideological struggle that called forth daring, courage, imagination, and idealism, will be replaced by economic calculation, the endless solving of technical problems, environmental concerns, and the satisfaction of sophisticated consumer demands. In the post-historical period there will be neither art nor philosophy, just the perpetual caretaking of the museum of the human spirit.¹⁰

But what did this amount to except, expressed in an unfamiliar idiom and emerging from an unexpected quarter, the central thesis of postmodernism, that the 'grand narratives' of human emancipation had become exhausted in the 'hyperreal' world of consumer capitalism, where struggles to transform society were supplanted by the simulation of experience through the agency of the mass media, whose images did not reflect but rather formed reality? In that respect, Fukuyama's 'Endism' was merely a variation on one of the dominant cultural themes of the 1980s.

The political implications were, however, plain enough: the West had won; socialism, at least in its Marxist form, was finished. The New Right, were naturally quick to trumpet this message. It would have been most surprising if they had not. Mrs Thatcher proclaimed the 1980s the decade of 'the failure of socialism'. One of her strongest intellectual supporters, Lord Rees-Mogg, ex-editor of *The Times*, announced with the air of someone who had made a new discovery that 'Marx is a dead prophet. He is kaput', though it was hard to imagine that he had ever believed anything different.[11] Another ardent Thatcherite, Paul Johnson, sought to use the East European revolutions to drum up support for a witch-hunt, in the process revealing the profoundly libertarian commitments of the New Right:

> What is surprising, in the Britain of the 1990s, is that the intellectual followers of this dangerous charlatan [viz. Marx] should still have an influential voice in our press, on our airwaves and in our academia. We would not permit such licence to exponents of Nazi race-theory. Marxism is mortally wounded, but there is no reason it should enjoy the luxury of a prolonged death-bed scene.[12]

Even a more complex and interesting figure, Timothy Garton Ash, could not resist milking the revolutions in the hope of reviving the flagging fortunes of the Western New Right. Ash covered as a journalist the birth and initial defeat of Solidarność in 1980–1, when, in John Rees's felicitous phrase, he was 'touched by the lightning finger of revolution'.[13] His dispatches in *The Spectator* and subsequent book, *The Polish Revolution*, captured brilliantly the great Polish workers' movement in all its life and contradictions. Every flurry of resistance in the East, faithfully and vividly recorded by Ash, was used, however, to hammer home the same message – the only alternative to Stalinism was Western liberal capitalism. Ash's description of Dubček's return to Prague in November 1989 illustrates alike his literary flair, his eye for detail and gift for the telling analogy, and his hostility to socialism:

> As we scuttled along the covered shopping arcades to reach the balcony, people simply gaped. It was as if the ghost of Winston Churchill were to be seen striding down the Burlington Arcade. But when he stepped out into the frosty evening air, illuminated by television lights, the crowd gave such a roar as I have never heard. 'DUBČEK! DUBČEK!' ... He has not changed with the times. His speeches still contain those wooden, prefabricated newspeak phrases. He still believes in socialism – that is, reformed communism, with a human face.[14]

Presumably if Dubček had instead treated the crowd to a lecture in the voodoo economics of Hayek and Friedman – as did the considerably more compromised figure of Valtr Komarek, who somehow managed to extricate himself from Communist Party membership and become First Deputy Prime Minister under Havel – Ash would have sagely praised him for his wisdom.

All this was, however, to be expected. More interesting, perhaps, was the revolutions' impact on what one might call the left-liberal intelligentsia. One does not have to accept the kind of conspiracy theory favoured by the likes of Paul Johnson to recognize that in Britain at least those involved in purveying ideas and other forms of high-cultural activity have, at any rate since the 1960s, had their political sympathies to the left of centre: hence, for example, the hostility with which the Thatcher government was generally received by them. It may be that the collapse of the Stalinist regimes has promoted a sea-change in the opinions of this group. One highly suggestive occasion was Salman Rushdie's Herbert Read lecture, delivered *in absentia* on 6 February 1990. Rushdie's plight had, understandably, made him something of a liberal hero. The lecture was, again understandably, a manifesto for the kind of Modernist art practised so well by Rushdie in his novels. But, whereas he had previously seemed to endorse a politically engaged art, to be a writer of the left, Rushdie now defended literature as a more abstract form of scepticism, the constant subversion of established orthodoxies and dominant languages. In a keynote passage he linked this conception of literature to the East European revolutions:

> It seems probable ... that we may be heading towards a world in which there will be no real alternative to the liberal-capitalist social model ... In this situation, liberal capitalism or democracy or the free world will require novelists' most rigorous attention, will require re-imagining and questioning and doubting as never before. 'Our antagonist is our helper,' said Edmund Burke, and if democracy no longer has communism to help it clarify, by opposition, its own ideas, then perhaps it will have to have literature as an adversary instead.[15]

Many others shared this sense that the upheavals in the East marked a *closure* of alternatives. An example is provided by the New York economist Robert Heilbroner, who long occupied a position mid-way between Marxism and liberalism. In the 1970s he had written books with such titles as *Business Civilization in Decline* and predicted a 'shift ... to economic planning, the only institutional transformation that can, in my opinion, give a new measure of life, albeit a limited one, to the capitalist system'.[16] But in January 1989, even before the great events in Eastern Europe, Heilbroner announced: 'Less than 75 years after it officially began, the contest between capitalism and socialism is over; capitalism has won ... the great question now seems how rapid will be the transformation of socialism into capitalism, and not the other way around.'[17]

This kind of judgement found echoes from those with far more substantial Marxist credentials than Heilbroner's. The historian Eric Hobsbawm had been the chief intellectual ornament of the Communist Party of Great Britain (CPGB) and its journal *Marxism Today*. His faith in the USSR had survived such tests as the bloody suppression of the Hungarian Revolution in 1956, which drove other distinguished historians – for example, Edward Thompson, Christopher Hill, and John Saville – out of the party. Now it cracked. The Soviet Union 'obviously wasn't a workers' state, and nobody in the Soviet Union ever believed it was a workers' state, and the workers knew it wasn't a workers' state', Hobsbawm said. He went further:

> What's happening now is the final liquidation of the era of catastrophe, which spread over the entire world with the breakdown of liberal capitalism. For about half a century, from 1917 to the aftermath of the Second World War, the world passed through a period of cataclysm, producing all manner of freak results, of which the Russian Revolution is probably the most long-lasting. Sometime in the 1950s, ... the world-system appeared to get back onto an even keel. From then on, the situation has been completely different.[18]

Other Communists were prepared to go further than dismissing the Russian Revolution as a 'freak result' or (as Hobsbawm also called it) a 'detour'. Chris Myant, the CPGB International Secretary, declared:

> October 1917, the world event which separates communists from others on the left, was a mistake of truly historic proportions.
>
> Its consequences have been severe. They have characterized and moulded the great traumas of the 20th century: a second world war; Hitler's gas chambers; Stalin's gulag; the world of the show trials; the perpetuation of third world fascist dictatorships; the unprecedented, almost unbelievable waste of the arms race in a world of poverty and starvation; the destruction of the Vietnam War ...[19]

A formidable bill of indictment indeed – though one might think that the West had got off remarkably lightly, having been apparently absolved of any responsibility even for the Vietnam war. If the

October Revolution had been such a disaster, then there seemed little point in the existence of separate Communist Parties. *Marxism Today* editor Martin Jacques spelled out this conclusion to the CPGB congress in November 1989: 'The international communist movement is now surely at an end.'[20] What the minuscule and declining British CP did was of little real significance, though Hobsbawm's and Jacques's pronouncements did allow the media to confirm that even, as it were, the official representatives of Marxism accepted that it was dead. Elsewhere, much more powerful forces were on the move. Above all, the Italian Communist Party, the largest and most important of the Western CPs, voted in March 1990 to transform itself into a broad social-democratic party under a different name.

This process – the evolution of the Communist Parties into social-democratic organizations – was, of course, a long-term affair, having its origins in the Popular Front era of the 1930s and surfacing dramatically with the rise of Eurocommunism in the 1970s. Moreover, the disillusionment of the left intelligentsia with Marxism could be traced back over more than a decade, to the emergence of the *nouveaux philosophes* in a Paris demoralized by the disappointment of the hopes raised by 1968. The impact of the East European revolutions was thus in large part to accelerate well-established trends. There were, however, changes which they seem to have independently promoted. The South African Communist Party (SACP) was one of the very few to experience at the end of the 1980s a growth in size and influence, especially in the new black workers' movement largely organized through the Congress of South African Trade Unions. The SACP was also a profoundly Stalinist party both in ideology and in organizational practices. In January 1990 SACP Secretary-General Joe Slovo issued a discussion paper called *Has Socialism Failed?* in which he abruptly dumped the ideological baggage of sixty years, denouncing the USSR's systematic deviation until Gorbachev from the principles of Marx and Lenin, but set the party firmly on a course which seemed, once again, to take it towards social democracy.

The haste of such changes suggests that they should be regarded with a degree of suspicion. After all, the revelations which *glasnost* permitted about the crimes of the Stalin regime – collectivization, the camps, the Terror – merely confirmed what had been known to the few who bothered to look in the 1930s, and had been documented in the era after Khrushchev's 1956 secret speech in works of such different ideological provenance as Robert Conquest's *The Great Terror*, Roy Medvedev's *Let History Judge*, and Aleksandr Solzhenitsyn's

The Gulag Archipelago. Stalinism's *moral* bankruptcy had been evident for a generation at least. What had changed was the erosion, indeed progressive collapse, of Stalinism as a system of *power*. George Orwell had long ago stressed the element of power worship in the Western intelligentsia's love affair with the Soviet Union. This attitude had, it seemed, survived into the 1980s, only to encourage the rearrangement of political loyalties once the practical failure of the Stalinist regimes to provide an alternative centre of power to the West was established beyond any doubt.

Even many Western socialists who had not been implicated in collaboration within Stalinism drew apocalyptic – and usually gloomy – conclusions from the East European revolutions. *New Left Review*, generally regarded as the premier journal of Marxist theory, had tended to follow Isaac Deutscher in viewing the Stalinist regimes as a distorted expression of revolutionary impulses: thus, while supporting anti-bureaucratic movements in the Soviet bloc, *NLR* gave its critical support to the East against the West in what it regarded as the 'Great Contest' between capitalism and communism. It therefore could not avoid seeing the East European revolutions as a historic setback for the left. Fred Halliday described the end of the Cold War as 'nothing less than the defeat of the communist project as it has been known in the twentieth century and the triumph of the capitalist'. 'The greatest mistake of Marxist and socialist thinking,' he argued, was 'the underestimation of capitalism', which in the West at any rate 'enjoyed an unparalleled period of growth in the postwar epoch', and extended its hegemony through both greater popular acceptance of liberal democracy and the expansion of a commodified mass culture. The 'reassessment of classical Marxism' consequently required, Halliday concluded, should include a return to the eight-eenth-century Enlightenment as the best response to 'the resurgent challenges of the time, clericalism, nationalism and irrationalism'.[21]

Left and right seemed thus to agree on the moral of the East European revolutions: capitalism has triumphed and Marxism, if not quite finished, is in what may well turn out to be a terminal crisis. Those with qualms about the virtues of unregulated capitalism could at best, like the veteran Polish dissident Adam Michnik, advocate 'the market with a human face'.[22] This, in any case, had become the programme of Western social democracy: 1989 saw the British Labour Party under Neil Kinnock fall in line with its Continental counterparts and adopt the objective of making the market more efficient and humane than it would be if presided over by the likes of Thatcher and Bush. Rather than offer an alternative to Western liberal democracy, socialists should work within its framework to remedy the dysfunctions and injustices of unfettered capitalism. The idea of socialism as an alternative socio-economic *system*, a mode of production in Marxist parlance, was gone.

1.3 MARXISM *CONTRA* STALINISM

This line of reasoning is persuasive only if one is ready to equate Marxism and Stalinism. It is necessary here to be more precise. I say much more about Marxism below. By 'Stalinism' I mean, not one person's rule or even a body of beliefs, but the whole system of social power that crystallized in the USSR in the 1930s, was exported to Eastern Europe in the second half of the 1940s, and survived till the late 1980s when it began to collapse, a system characterized by the hierarchically organized control of all aspects of social life, political, economic, and cultural, by a narrow oligarchy seated at the apex of the party and state apparatuses, the *nomenklatura*. The equation then involves the claim that this system of power is the practical realization of Marxism as a political tradition. This equation tends to imply another, namely: Marxism = Leninism = Stalinism. The apostolic (or diabolic) succession thus established involves tracing a direct line of political continuity between Marx's own theoretical and strategic conceptions, the Bolshevik political project which triumphed in October 1917, and the final shape assumed by the post-revolutionary regime in the 1930s. There have, of course, been many attempts to challenge these equations, to argue, for example, that Lenin betrayed Marx's own aspirations. It is, nevertheless, very striking to what extent both opponents and supporters of the USSR have since the 1930s agreed in seeing a continuity connecting Marx and Lenin to Stalinism. They have differed chiefly over whether they approved of the end result. Even after 1956, orthodox Communists have tended to treat the Stalinist Terror as 'excesses' attributable to 'the cult of personality' and therefore as marring rather than negating what they believed to be the successful construction of socialism in the USSR under Stalin: this broad historical interpretation was indeed defended by Gorbachev as recently as his speech marking the seventieth anniversary of the October Revolution in November 1987. To a large extent the ideological crisis surveyed in the previous section involves previously loyal Communists such as Hobsbawm preserving the original equation ('Marxism = Leninism = Stalinism') but now putting a minus rather than a plus sign against it. Where once Marx and Lenin were praised because their ideas had been so triumphantly realized in 'actually existing socialism', now they are damned for having promoted a movement that has ended so disastrously.

The supposed continuity underlying such praise and condemnation alike cannot be sustained. A qualitative break separates Stalinism from Marx and Lenin. This profound discontinuity can be traced in the historical record, in the process which transformed the Bolshevik Party, even in the 1920s still what Moshe Lewin calls an 'alliance of factions' rather than the monolith of liberal and Stalinist myth, into the apparatus of power, terrorized and terrorizing, that it became by the end of the 1930s.[23] It was a transformation which evoked resistance, notably from Lenin himself during the last months of his active political life in late 1922 and early 1923.[24] Other Bolshevik leaders contributed to the destruction of the traditions of inner-party dissent and debate through their alliances with Stalin during the faction-fights of the 1920s, till they started back in horror at the monster they had helped to create – a process vividly illustrated by the famous meeting in July 1928, when Bukharin, the defeated leader of the Right faction, told his former opponent Kamenev that Stalin was 'a Genghis Khan' who 'will cut our throats'.[25] One grouping alone consistently combated Stalinism from 1923 onwards, Trotsky and the Left Opposition. For this they paid a terrible price, Trotsky murdered in exile by a Russian agent, his supporters mainly perishing in the Gulag, where they were one of the few groups actively to organize resistance to the camp regime.[26] Nevertheless, the existence of the Trotskyist tradition, though largely extirpated in the USSR and confined to the margins of the labour movement in the West, is of capital importance, since it indicates that commitment to revolutionary socialism is not equivalent to endorsement of Stalinism.

More than that, this anti-Stalinist continuation of the classical Marxist tradition provides the basis for a socialist response to the East European revolutions. Far from being disconfirmed by the collapse of the Stalinist regimes, Marxism, understood in these terms, is an indispensable means of making sense of them. Marxism is relevant here in three different dimensions. First, Marx constructed what was fundamentally a theory of social transformation. Historical materialism explains the rise and fall of social formations in terms of the underlying conflict that develops between the forces and relations of production and of the class struggle rooted in exploitive social relations which this conflict intensifies. Marx, of course, concentrated on the analysis of one specific socio-economic system, the capitalist mode of production, an analysis deepened and extended by later classical Marxists. One of the most important features of the intellectual revival of Marxism since the late 1960s has been the considerable conceptual refinement and empirical elaboration of historical materialism as a *general* theory of the development and transformation of all societies, pre-capitalist as well as capitalist.[27]

Even Marxism's opponents have been forced grudgingly to acknowledge its continued salience, as did Ernest Gellner when he wrote:

> Whether or not people positively believe in the Marxist scheme, no coherent, well-articulated rival pattern has emerged, West or East; as people must needs think against some kind of grid, even (or perhaps especially) those who do not accept the Marxist theory of history tend to lean upon its ideas when they wish to say what they do positively believe.[28]

Indeed, one of the principal trends in English-speaking social theory during the 1980s was precisely such an implicit tribute, namely the formulation of various ambitious 'historical sociologies', which sought to offer, like Marxism, a general account of historical change, but which tended to give ideological movements and political and military conflicts the same explanatory importance as contradictions between the forces and relations of production.[29] Historical materialism has thus demonstrated its intellectual vitality, its capacity to set the theoretical agenda. A theory distinguished precisely by its focus on epochal transformations should be well equipped to interpret the progressive collapse of the Stalinist regimes.

But Marxism is, of course, much more than a powerful, historically oriented social theory; from Marx's time onwards, it has defined a political project of human emancipation. This is the second dimension in which Marxism is relevant to the East European revolutions. Marx developed a highly particular conception of socialism, as the self-emancipation of the working class: 'The emancipation of the working class must be achieved by the working class itself.'[30] This involves, in the first instance, a specific claim about the *agency* of socialist transformation: the exploited class in capitalist society, collectivized by the very conditions of production it experiences, has the interest and capacity and will develop the organization and consciousness required to inaugurate a classless society. At the same time, however, Marx's conception of socialism implies a particular view of the *process of transformation* itself. Socialism is not something which can be achieved on behalf of the working class by some group acting in its name, whether it be a Stalinist 'vanguard' or social-democratic parliamentarians. 'The proletarian movement,' Marx says, 'is the self-conscious independent movement of the immense majority, in the interest of the immense majority.'[31] His is a conception, in Hal Draper's words, of 'socialism from below', springing from the self-activity of the masses themselves.[32] This view of socialist revolution informs Marx's analysis of the Paris Commune of 1871, which concentrates on the dismantling of the bureaucratic state machine by the working people of Paris and its replacement by organs of popular self-government. It is developed by Lenin in *The State and Revolution*, one of whose main themes is the emergence during the Russian Revolutions of 1905 and 1917 of the soviets, councils of factory delegates, which he argued represented the basis of the radically democratic 'Commune-State' that would act as the political framework of the transition to a communist society without classes or a state.

It is this conception of socialism that I employ in this book. The discrepancy between it and the 'really existing socialism' that used to prevail in the USSR and Eastern bloc is all too evident. By this measure, it was not socialism which went into its death agonies in the late 1980s. Thus identifying socialism with the classical Marxist conception of the self-emancipation of the working class may seem like a defensive manoeuvre, an attempt to dissociate the revolutionary socialist tradition from the catastrophe in the East. This accusation fails, however, to strike home. In the first place, it is just a matter of fact that there is a demonstrable difference between Marx's − and Lenin's − conception of socialism and the theory and practice of the Stalinist regimes. It is an entirely appropriate response to right-wing polemic to insist on that difference. Secondly, as my reference to Lenin indicates, it was this conception of socialism which informed the strategies and interventions of those who actually led the October Revolution. It is an entirely legitimate form of historical interpretation to appraise the outcome of that Revolution in terms of its makers' self-understanding. The result of such an appraisal need not be favourable to classical Marxism: it might turn out to be true that, as many of its more intelligent critics have argued, the very attempt to carry through a radically democratic revolution oriented towards a classless and stateless society, by setting itself Utopian objectives, helped to bring about the Stalinist despotism that reversed the original revolution. Making Marx's and Lenin's views the benchmark of socialism does not therefore prejudge the issue in their favour.

There is, moreover, a third respect in which the classical Marxist tradition is relevant to understanding the East European revolutions.

For that tradition gave birth to the first systematic attempt at a social and historical analysis of Stalinism. Trotsky's *The Revolution Betrayed* (1937) pioneered that analysis by locating the origins of the Stalin phenomenon in the conditions of material scarcity prevailing in the Civil War of 1918–21, in which the bureaucracy of party officials began to develop. He concluded that the USSR was a 'degenerated workers' state', in which the bureaucracy had succeeded in politically expropriating the proletariat but left the social and economic foundations of workers' power untouched. The contradictions of that analysis, according to which the workers were still the ruling class of a state which denied them all political power, did not prevent Trotsky's more dogmatic followers extending it to China and Eastern Europe, even though the result was to break any connection between socialism and the self-emancipation of the working class: socialism, it seemed, could be imposed by the Red Army or peasant guerillas.[33] The Palestinian Trotskyist Tony Cliff refused, however, to accept this line of reasoning. Trotsky's insistence on treating the USSR as a workers' state, despite the dominance of the Stalinist bureaucracy, reflected, according to Cliff, the illicit conflation of the legal form of state ownership of the means of production with the relations of production proper, in which the working class was excluded from any effective control of the productive forces. The USSR and its replicants in China and Eastern Europe were, he argued, bureaucratic state-capitalist societies, in which the bureaucracy collectively fulfilled the role performed under private capitalism by the bourgeoisie of extracting surplus-value and directing the accumulation process.

This analysis, first developed by Cliff in 1947 in what became the basis of his book *State Capitalism in Russia*, provides, in my view, the best framework for understanding the nature and evolution of the Stalinist regimes. In particular, Cliff's theory allowed him to predict that these regimes would be brought down by the working class in whose name they ruled. 'The class struggle in Stalinist Russia', he wrote in 1947, '*must inevitably* express itself in gigantic spontaneous outbursts of millions', which would be 'the first chapter in the victorious proletarian revolution'.[34] At the end of the 1960s Chris Harman gave this perspective a more concrete form, when he analysed the dilemma posed for the Stalinist regimes by the pressures for reform represented by the Prague Spring:

> If reforms, in collaboration with foreign capital or otherwise, are not carried through . . . , the chronic crisis of the Russian and East European economies can only grow worse . . . Yet it is also increasingly

clear that the bureaucracy is unable to carry through reforms on anything like a successful basis without a split of the proportions that characterized Hungary in 1956 and Czechoslovakia in early 1968. Such a split could only be the prelude to an immense crisis throughout the USSR and Eastern Europe, in which the extra-bureaucratic classes would mobilize behind their own demands.[35]

Twenty years later that 'immense crisis' finally exploded. The East European revolutions and the turmoil in the USSR itself are thus the vindication, rather than the refutation, of the classical Marxist tradition as it has been continued by those who have sought to develop a historical materialist analysis of Stalinism itself. This claim can only be established satisfactorily by considering the October Revolution and its fate, to which I now turn.

2

THE *ANCIEN RÉGIME* AND THE REVOLUTION

'Beginning reform is beginning revolution.'
Arthur Wellesley, First Duke of Wellington

2.1 REVOLUTION AND COUNTER-REVOLUTION

An acceptable account of the Russian Revolution of October 1917 must be able satisfactorily to connect its causes, nature, and consequences. The standard version accepted these days by both right and left tends to run all three together. It goes something like this. The October Revolution was an aberration (recall Hobsbawm's words a 'freak result'): a chance constellation of circumstances reflecting more the hazards of war than the long-term trends of Russian social development allowed the Bolsheviks to seize power. However, the methods used by Lenin and his supporters first to achieve and then to maintain control of the state brought into being the Stalinist system, in which power was centralized in the hands of the *nomenklatura* at the top of the party-state apparatus. Though many Bolsheviks may have been horrified by the final outcome of their own deeds, the 'Stalin revolution' of the late 1920s and 1930s was at once the fulfilment and the consolidation of the regime created by Lenin's coup. Among historians there are variations in emphasis. Some seek to ascertain the authoritarian trends in pre-revolutionary society, traceable perhaps as far back as the semi-Asiatic context in which the mediaeval Muscovite monarchy emerged, which prepared the way for the Bolshevik despotism.[1] Others, less willing to see the Revolution as some kind of malign throwback, nevertheless regard 'the February and October Revolutions of 1917, the Civil War, the interlude of NEP and Stalin's First Five-Year Plan revolution as successive stages in a single process'.[2] Most versions tend, at the very least, to underline the continuity typically posited between the Bolshevik Revolution and the Stalinist system to which it finally gave issue.

Now, in the first place, it just seems wrong to regard the 1917 Revolution as an accident. This interpretation leaves out of account the extent to which the entire European state-system was thrown into a *general* crisis towards the end of the First World War. In some ways the most striking episode in this crisis was not the Russian Revolution itself but the succession of upheavals that convulsed the most advanced European power, Germany, for almost five years, from the Revolution of November 1918 which overthrew the Kaiser to the Communist Party's abortive attempt to seize power in October 1923 in the wake of the great inflation of that year.[3] The victorious powers were also affected: 1919 was arguably the most dangerous year the British state has faced since the days of the Chartists, while Italy experienced the *biennio rosso* culminating in the factory occupations of September 1920.[4] It was during the First World War that Bukharin formulated the fullest version of the Marxist theory of imperialism, explaining the military rivalries of the Great Powers in terms of the tendency towards the concentration and centralization of capital which found its highest expression in a trend towards state capitalism: economic competition between firms was now being supplanted by armed conflict between 'state-capitalist trusts'.[5]

From this perspective, the Russia of Nicholas II was, in Lenin's famous phrase, 'the weakest link in the imperialist chain', the most serious victim of a disease shared by all the Great Powers. The social tensions making the Tsarist regime especially vulnerable were analysed by Trotsky in the aftermath of the 1905 Revolution. Russia exemplified what he would later call 'uneven and combined development'. Impelled by its military rivalries with the more advanced states of Central and Western Europe to promote, in alliance with foreign capital, the rapid industrialization of Russia, the Romanov autocracy found itself by the turn of the nineteenth century faced with a society in which the traditional conflicts between lord and peasant, intelligentsia and state were intensified by the contradiction between capital and labour. The 'advantage of backwardness' allowed Russia to import the most advanced industrial technology available, which led to the headlong emergence of a working class concentrated in some of the largest and most modern factories in the world but, thanks to its lack of even the most elementary rights to organize to improve its wretched material conditions, without the reformist inhibitions already being developed by the Western labour movement. This volatile combination of advanced and backward, Trotsky predicted on the basis of the 'dress rehearsal' of 1905, would allow this industrial proletariat to exercise an influence out of proportion to its numbers (3.3 million out of an economically active population of 30.6 million in 1897), and lead the mass of smallholding peasants in a revolution against, not merely Tsarism, but capitalism itself.[6]

The two revolutions of 1917 could thus be seen, in the light of Trotsky's prognosis, as the result of a crisis of authoritarian modernization, precipitated by the destabilizing impact on a predominantly feudal and rural social order of capitalist industrialization and intensified by the First World War, itself the product of the interstate rivalries which had encouraged the state-imposed transformation of Russian society in the first place. But this analysis does not explain why the Bolsheviks were the chief beneficiary of this crisis. Bolshevism was the result of the confluence of three distinct currents: the Russian revolutionary tradition, forged in the course of the nineteenth century by an intelligentsia radicalized by the contrast between the aspirations they formed with the help of Western political and social theory, and the Tsarist bureaucracy to which most owed their existence; classical Marxism, the last of the succession of theories imported from the West and adapted to fit Russian conditions by *intelligenty* eager to make sense of, and transform, their situation; and the workers' movement stimulated by the sufferings produced by industrialization and which in 1905 baptized with the name 'soviet' what was to prove to be the characteristic organizational form of working-class insurrection.

The first of these three factors is often said to have over-determined the other two: the conspiratorial techniques of the terrorist Narodnaya Volya were given canonical form in Lenin's *What is to be Done?* (1902), and laid the basis for the Bolshevik coup in October 1917. This claim does not sit well with the actual history of the Bolshevik Party: the tight hierarchical structures advocated by Lenin in 1902 were abandoned during the 1905 Revolution; then, and again during the great wave of proletarian militancy in 1912–14, the Bolsheviks became a mass working-class party responsive to all the currents of opinion within the factories.[7] The same pattern was repeated in 1917 itself. N. N. Sukhanov, one of the first and best historians of the Revolution, was a Menshevik-Internationalist bitterly hostile to the Bolshevik strategy of overturning the Provisional Government established in February 1917 and replacing it with a soviet regime. Yet he summarily dismissed the theory, still widely held, that the insurrection of 25 October which brought the Bolsheviks to power was a 'military conspiracy':

was the Petersburg proletariat in sympathy or not with the organizers of the October insurrection? . . . Here there can be no two replies. Yes, the Bolsheviks acted with the full backing of the Petersburg workers and soldiers. And they brought about an insurrection, throwing into it as many (very few!) forces as were required for its successful consummation.[8]

Recent historical research has lent strong support to Sukhanov's judgement. Thus Alexander Rabinowitch's studies of the Bolshevik Party in Petrograd (St Petersburg) during 1917 reveal an organization very different from the hierarchically controlled monolith supposedly required by Leninist doctrine. On the contrary, 'amid the chaotic, locally varying, constantly fluctuating conditions prevailing in Russia in 1917, the Central Committee, at the top of the Bolshevik organizational hierarchy, was simply unable to control the behaviour of major regional organizations. Except in a broad way, it rarely tried.' Rabinowitch argues that 'the relative flexibility of the party, as well as its responsiveness to the prevailing mass mood, had at least as much to do with the ultimate Bolshevik victory as did revolutionary discipline, organizational unity, or obedience to Lenin'.[9] The vitality of internal debate affected all levels of the party: Central Committee members frequently differed openly, and Lenin often found himself in a minority on such crucial issues as the party's strategy of opposition to the Provisional Government, the decision to organize the October insurrection itself, and, after the seizure of power, the Brest-Litovsk Treaty of February 1918.[10] Marc Ferro, whose social history of the Revolution is generally hostile to the Bolsheviks, nevertheless concedes that 'a challenging of institutions and a radicalization of opinion and behaviour' among workers, soldiers, peasants, and subject nationalities alike allowed the Bolsheviks to give 'direction to a movement that was both incoherent and convergent – the will to overthrow the regime'.[11] Decisive to this process was the industrial working class, from whose ranks was drawn the bulk of the Bolsheviks' membership (which rose tenfold to 240,000 between February and August 1917), and whose extensive self-organization, in factory committees, trade unions and soviets, provided the basis of the October insurrection: indeed, the demand for action in the factories at times outdistanced the Bolshevik leaders themselves, for example during the July Days in Petrograd.

There is thus, on the face of things, a profound *discontinuity* between the October Revolution and the Stalinist regime it was later used to legitimize. How did a revolution whose driving force was provided by popular, especially proletarian, pressures from below so lose its way? The standard account finds the answer in Bolshevik ideology and organizational practices. But how does this square with the reality of the Bolshevik Party at the time of the Revolution, in Moshe Lewin's words, 'an authentic party of the urban masses, a legal democratic party made up of people from diverse social strata and heterogeneous ideological horizons'?[12] Even supposing we grant that some Bolshevik policies and methods helped prepare the way for the Stalin regime, these words of Victor Serge, a critical, libertarian supporter of first the Bolsheviks and then the Left Opposition, retain their pertinence:

> It is often said that 'the germ of all Stalinism was in Bolshevism at its beginning'. Well, I have no objection. Only, Bolshevism also contained many other germs − a mass of other germs − and those who lived through the enthusiasm of the first years of the first victorious revolution ought not to forget it. To judge the living man by the death germs which the autopsy reveals in a corpse − and which he may have carried with him since his birth − is this very sensible?[13]

Serge's metaphor suggests that attention should be paid chiefly to the historical circumstances which promoted the transformation of soviet democracy into an authoritarian regime. Fundamental among these was the economic collapse. Food shortages, layoffs, and factory closures helped to promote the radicalization in 1917 itself; workers in particular responded to what they saw as a conscious strategy of economic sabotage, summed up by the notorious call by the liberal industrialist Ryabushinsky on capitalists 'to employ the bony arm of hunger, and of national misery − to take these false friends of the people, the committees and the soviets − by the throat'.[14] The outbreak of civil war in the summer of 1918 and the imposition of a blockade by the Western Allies turned a desperate situation into a catastrophe. Starved of inputs, industry contracted drastically. The urban working class shrank as factories closed and workers fled the cities in search of food. The number of industrial workers fell from 3,024,000 in 1917 to 1,243,000 in 1921−2. The change was most dramatic in Petrograd, the capital of the Revolution: there were only 71,575 factory workers employed in the city in April 1918 compared to 400,000 the previous October.[15] The transformation of the working class was qualitative as well as quantitative: as David Mandel notes, '[t]he factories lost the bulk of their most active and radical elements − the young workers and the Bolsheviks, who had emerged as the workers' natural leaders in the course of the revolution', and many of whom now went to serve the new state as soldiers in the Red Army or public officials.[16]

The Bolshevik Party thus found itself ruling in the name of a proletariat at best a shadow of the class which made the October Revolution. At the same time, fighting for its survival in the Civil War of 1918–21, the new regime resorted increasingly to coercion as the main way in which to govern society. The moderate socialist parties which had supported the Provisional Government, the Mensheviks and Social Revolutionaries, were suppressed as they sided with the Whites in the Civil War. The Bolsheviks matched their opponents' use of terror with their own, organized by what became a new secret police, the Cheka. Grain was forcibly extracted from the peasantry by armed food detachments from the cities. Industry, contrary to Lenin's original intentions, was nationalized to prevent complete collapse. The Bolsheviks made a virtue out of necessity under what came to be known as 'war communism', equating the state controls and rationing dictated by an appalling economic situation with the measures required to prepare the way for their ultimate objective of a society without classes or a state. Finally, the party itself was transformed into a bureaucratically organized apparatus in which power flowed down from the top through the network of secretaries who, themselves now appointed rather than elected, increasingly controlled the composition of local committees and congress delegations.[17]

Marx had argued in *The German Ideology* that 'communism is only possible as the act of the dominant peoples "all at once" and simultaneously, which presupposes the universal development of productive forces', since 'without it privation, *want* is merely made general, and with *want* the struggle for necessities would begin again, and all the old filthy business would necessarily be restored'.[18] The Bolsheviks indeed never imagined that they could build socialism in Russia, most backward of the Great Powers, with a predominantly peasant population. Their strategy in seizing power was based on the expectation that the October insurrection was merely the first stage in a global revolutionary process. Thus Lenin declared in January 1918 that 'the final victory of socialism in a single country is of course impossible' and that 'without a German revolution we are doomed.'[19] His anticipation of international revolution was far from irrational: October 1917 was, as we have already seen, merely the high point of a more general upheaval at the end of the First World War. The German Revolution of 1918–23 in particular was, despite its ultimate failure, a close-run thing. The Communist International, launched by

Bolsheviks in March 1919 with the aim of spreading the revolution to
the more advanced capitalist countries, rapidly succeeded in winning
a sizeable minority of the Western labour movement to its ranks.[20]

The fact remained that the Bolshevik regime, despite all its efforts
and the social and political convulsions experienced by postwar
Europe, did not succeed in breaking out of its isolation. It emerged
from the Civil War victorious, but presiding over a shattered economy and an increasingly hostile peasant majority. The fact that the
Bolsheviks were the only party in 1917 to support peasant seizures of
the estates of the gentry allowed them, as Lenin put it, to 'neutralize
the peasantry', securing at least their acquiescence in the October
Revolution.[21] Peasants' fear that the Whites would bring the land-
owners back was a decisive factor in the Bolsheviks' victory in the Civil
War. But the revolutionary land settlement greatly increased the
social and economic weight of peasant smallholders: the number of
family holdings rose from 17–18 million before 1917 to 23 million in
1923. Of the three rural social categories rather arbitrarily distinguished by Marxist analysts, the middle peasant reliant on family
labour on his own holding grew in importance relative to the
quasi-capitalist kulak and semi-proletarian poor peasant.[22] Bolshevik
policies, notably their attempt to suppress the grain trade and to feed
the towns by forcible exactions from the peasantry, helped alienate a
rural population already predisposed to regard with suspicion a
regime whose commitment to collective ownership seemed to
threaten their smallholdings.[23]

Lenin acknowledged the Bolsheviks' plight in January 1921: 'What
we actually have is a workers' state, with this peculiarity, firstly, that
it is not the working class but the peasant population that predomin-
ates in the country, and, secondly, that it is a workers' state with
bureaucratic distortions.'[24] It was also a state apparently on the verge
of being engulfed by mass unrest – strikes in Petrograd, a bitter
peasant rising in Tambov province, and the mutiny of the garrison of
the key naval base at Kronstadt. While this last revolt was being
suppressed in March 1921, the Tenth Party Congress adopted the
New Economic Policy (NEP), designed to conciliate the peasantry by
material concessions. Crucially, forced requisitions were abandoned,
state controls relaxed, and market mechanisms revived. Presented by
Lenin as a temporary retreat 'in view of the delay of the world
revolution', NEP permitted an unexpectedly rapid economic recovery
to pre-war levels of output.[25]

The longer-term course of the Bolshevik regime remained open,
however, and was the central issue in the bitter disputes within the

party leadership after illness removed Lenin from any active political role nearly two years before his death in January 1924. These struggles pitted Trotsky and the Left Opposition against Stalin in alliance first with Zinoviev and Kamenev, and then with Bukharin. It was Bukharin who actually formulated the doctrine of 'Socialism in One Country', though the assertion of national self-reliance it implied fitted more the outlook of the hard-headed party officials led by Stalin as General Secretary, impatient as they had become with the apparently vain hope of world revolution. Bukharin's most distinctive contribution as leader of the party Right was to argue that NEP should become the permanent framework of building socialism, even if this meant industrialization 'at a snail's pace' and promoting the development of private agriculture. 'Get rich', he told the peasants in April 1925. Trotsky and his supporters attacked this policy on the grounds that it threatened the very existence of soviet power by encouraging capital accumulation by kulaks and the Nepmen, traders who profited by the growth of the private market after 1921. The Left Opposition advocated the more rapid growth of state-controlled heavy industry, not least because this would increase the social and economic weight of the urban working class and thereby permit the revival of democracy in party and soviets which was one of their main demands. Industrialization could be financed partly through greater Russian involvement in the world market, which would make possible foreign loans and increased export earnings, and by what the brilliant economist Preobazhensky called 'primitive socialist accumulation', the transfer of resources from the private to the state sector by means of taxation and unequal exchange between agriculture and industry. At the same time, however, Trotsky and his followers argued that the contradictions of the Soviet economy could not be solved within a national framework. They therefore bitterly attacked the doctrine of 'Socialism in One Country' and what they saw as its disastrous effects in producing a series of defeats for the Comintern, notably in China during the 1925–7 Revolution.[26]

It was, of course, neither the Left nor the Right which won the party struggles of the 1920s but rather the 'Centre' around Stalin. This faction most closely represented the interests of the *apparat* of party officials. Stalin exploited what Robert Daniels called 'the circular flow of power' between the General Secretary and his appointees in the apparatus which allowed him to control party congresses and thus to determine the composition of the leadership itself.[27] The increasingly monolithic character of the party was given symbolic sanction by the formal ban on factions at the Tenth

Congress in 1921, and by the posthumous cult of Lenin. Trotsky was the first Bolshevik leader to analyse the party bureaucracy as a social phenomenon, but he tended, mistakenly, to see the forces of petty capitalism – the kulaks and the Nepmen – as the main threat to the regime, failing to recognize that the bureaucracy was proceeding under Stalin's leadership to establish its political domination legitimized by 'Leninism', which was now transformed into an ideological system, and by the doctrine of 'Socialism in One Country' through which this layer asserted its distinctive interests.

The political triumph of the Stalin faction, completed by the defeat of Bukharin and the Right in 1928–9, was, however, only the preliminary to a further transformation of Russian society, the forced collectivization and industrialization of the USSR. These dramatic changes, driven through during the period of the First Five-Year Plan (1928–32), are sometimes described as a further instalment of revolution, as 'Stalin's Revolution'.[28] In fact, as Cliff argues, they mark the point at which the bureaucracy transformed itself into a ruling class collectively exploiting a vastly enlarged proletariat and systematically subjected to competitive pressures to accumulate capital. The 'Stalin revolution' was thus a *counter*-revolution, in which the remnants of the 'workers' state with bureaucratic distortions' surviving from October 1917 were destroyed and bureaucratic state capitalism was installed in their place.[29]

This counter-revolution is best understood under four interrelated aspects. The policy evolved by Stalin and his supporters between 1927 and 1929 of forcibly collectivizing agriculture formed the starting point of the entire process. A sharp fall in grain procurements in October 1927 sent NEP into its death agonies: the entire economy was soon affected, since the consequent fall in grain exports forced cutbacks in the import of raw materials and machinery required by industry. The regime claimed that a 'grain strike' organized by the kulaks was responsible for the crisis, though in fact the principal culprit seems to have been government policies which reduced the peasants' incentive to sell grain. In any case, the fall in procurements simply brought to a head a more general crisis. In May 1927 Britain broke off relations with the USSR, encouraging a war scare in Moscow. Moreover, the United Opposition led by Trotsky, Zinoviev, and Kamenev were able to capitalize on growing working-class discontent caused by the sharply increased unemployment endemic in the late NEP period. The latter threat was removed by the large-scale application of repression. Stalin resorted to the same remedy to resolve the procurements crisis, personally supervising in early 1928 the forcible seizure of grain from the peasantry in Siberia. The adoption of what came to be known as the 'Urals-Siberian' method marked Stalin's break with Bukharin and the Right, who conceded defeat in January 1929, having succumbed to the same methods they had helped use against Trotsky and his allies.[30]

The triumphant Stalin faction now groped towards turning what had been an emergency expedient into a general policy, of forcing the peasants to join collective farms: the summer of 1929 saw the party swing into action to implement 'mass collectivization', followed by the decision in December to proceed with the 'liquidation of the kulaks as a class'. Thus unfolded one of the most terrible crimes of the century. 'Kulak' proved to be a highly flexible category, expanding to include any peasant who resisted collectivization and was therefore declared a *podkulachnik*, 'kulak hireling'. Perhaps a million peasant households were deported to the slave-labour camps of the Gulag Archipelago. The peasants fought back in various ways, slaughtering livestock rather than hand them over to the state, and mounting risings in the North Caucasus and the Ukraine, for example. Ruthless coercion, however, overwhelmed all overt resistance. The state's share of the grain crop rose from 14.7 per cent in 1928 to 34.1 per cent five years later. This success was, however, bought at a terrible price: 1933 was a year of famine in much of the countryside, notably in the Ukraine. Some indication of the toll is given by the fact that the population of the USSR in 1939 was more than ten million below the figure projected from demographic information about the pre-1933 period.[31]

This process is only intelligible against the background of the regime's adoption of a policy of rapid industrialization, the second main aspect of the Stalin counter-revolution. The First Five-Year Plan, operative from October 1928 though only formally approved the following April and declared completed nearly a year early at the end of 1932, involved highly ambitious initial targets which were then revised upwards, so that on the 'optimal' variant of the Plan industrial production was to grow by 244.5 per cent over the four years.[32] Underlying this abrupt break with the much slower pace of industrialization under NEP was the fear of war with more advanced powers. Stalin spelled out the connection between the First Five-Year Plan and strategic concerns in his famous attack on critics of rapid industrialization in February 1931:

> To slacken the tempo would mean falling behind. And those who fall behind get beaten. But we do not want to get beaten. No, we refuse to

be beaten! One feature of the history of old Russia was the continual beatings she suffered because of her backwardness. She was beaten by the Mongol khans. She was beaten by the Turkish beys. She was beaten by the Swedish feudal lords. She was beaten by the Polish and Lithuanian gentry. She was beaten by the British and French capitalists. She was beaten by the Japanese barons. All beat her – because of her backwardness, because of her military backwardness, cultural backwardness, political backwardness, industrial backwardness, agricultural backwardness ... We are fifty or a hundred years behind the advanced countries. We must make good this distance in ten years. Either we do it, or we shall go under.[33]

This strategy can be seen as a response to the dilemma posed by Lenin in March 1919: 'We are living not merely in a state, but *in a system of states*, and it is inconceivable for the Soviet Republic to live alongside of the imperialist states for any length of time. One or other must triumph in the end.'[34] The conclusion which Lenin drew, and which Trotsky reiterated after his death, was to seek, through the Comintern, to extend the revolution to other countries. But the doctrine of 'Socialism in One Country' implied the subordination of the interests of the international revolutionary movement to those of the Russian state. Once the Bolshevik regime had ceased to rely on the world revolution, it could only cope with its precarious position within the international state-system by itself becoming a Great Power like the others. But such a role required the military equipment to match those of the major capitalist states. What William H. McNeill calls the 'industrialization of war' which began in the mid-nineteenth century made Great-Power status dependent on the existence of a heavy-industrial base capable of mass-producing modern weapons-systems.[35] Like the Tsarist autocracy forty years earlier, the Stalin regime responded to the military competition of the more advanced powers by industrializing at breakneck speed.

The Tsarist regime, however, had been able to attract foreign investment and loans to help finance the necessary imports of Western technology. Stalinist Russia could expect no such assistance, especially after Western capitalism had succumbed to the Great Depression of the 1930s. The industrialization of the USSR could only proceed by pursuing economic autarky. Many, including Preobazhensky himself at the Seventeenth Party Congress in 1934, believed that the resources for industrialization had been provided through 'primitive socialist accumulation': that is, 'by exploiting the peasants, by concentrating resources of the peasantry in the hands of the state'.[36] This explanation has, however, been challenged by recent research, which suggests that, if anything, there was a net transfer of resources from industry to agriculture in 1928–32, reflecting, among other factors, the huge rise in the price of food sold on the private market during those hungry years and the very considerable investments made by the state in agricultural machinery to replace the livestock slaughtered by the peasants.[37]

Collectivization did, however, make a contribution to Soviet industrialization. First, it allowed the regime drastically to increase grain exports and thereby to finance imports of plant and equipment from the West. Between 1928 and 1931 the USSR's sales of grain on foreign markets rose 56-fold.[38] This huge rise in exports was a consequence not merely of industrializing Russia's demand for advanced technology but also of the fall in world food prices caused by the Great Depression. The obverse of this great export drive was the famines of 1933–4. Secondly, collectivization, by pushing many peasants out of the countryside, provided the new factories with their workforce. The number of industrial workers rose from 3,124,000 in 1928 to 8,290,000 in 1940. Much of this increase came from peasants fleeing the horrors of the rural areas. Between 1926 and 1939 the cities grew by some thirty million people and their share of the urban population went up from 18 to 24 per cent. The pace of urbanization was astonishing: in 1931 alone 4.1 million peasants moved to the cities.[39] Finally, collectivization, by allowing the state to gain direct control of agricultural production, ensured that it could feed the rapidly growing cities.

If, however, there was no net transfer from agriculture to industry, where did the surplus required for the very high rate of accumulation of those years come from? The Soviet economic historian A. A. Barsov makes the remarkable claim that '[t]he chief burden lay on the working class'. Michael Ellman summarizes the results of Barsov's research thus: 'The source of the increase in accumulation in 1929–31 was the surplus obtained from the employment of additional workers in the urban sector at real wages less than those enjoyed by employed workers in 1928 plus the surplus obtained by reducing the real wages of those who had been employed in 1928.' Barsov calculated that the rate of surplus-value rose from 27 per cent in 1928 to 110 per cent in 1932.[40] Real wages in 1932 were at most 50 per cent of their 1928 level. If this analysis is correct, then 'socialist' industrialization in the USSR was made possible not simply by the destruction of the peasantry but by the intense exploitation of the very class which in theory ruled the country and was supposed to be the main beneficiary of the changes involved. In fact, the First Five-Year Plan saw a more general reduction in the position of the working class in the USSR. Despite the decline of soviet democracy after the Revolution, industrial workers under NEP possessed very considerable legal protection defended by trade unions which had some degree of autonomy of the state. All these safeguards were swept away after 1928. Faced with a catastrophic fall in their living standards and intensive pressures to speed up production, workers found ways of resisting. The rapid establishment of full employment helped to create endemic labour-discipline problems for the regime. Strikes were quite frequent in the period 1928–34, but, given the very harsh methods used to crush them, other forms of resistance were more popular – for example, go-slows ('Italian strikes'), job turnover (in 1930 the average worker changed jobs every eight months), absenteeism. Such indirect forms of struggle are typical of a working class atomized by state terror but possessing, thanks to conditions of labour shortage, some bargaining power: a very similar pattern was displayed by workers' resistance in Nazi Germany.[41]

The struggles between workers and the regime were one dimension of a more general feature of the USSR in the 1930s, the enormous social flux created by Stalin's policies. Moshe Lewin in a brilliant essay has described this '"quicksand" society', in which

> workers, administrators, specialists, party apparatus men, and, in great masses, peasants were all moving around and changing jobs, creating unwanted surpluses in some places and dearths in others, losing skills or failing to acquire them, creating streams and floods in which families were destroyed, children lost, and morality dissolved. Social, administrative, industrial, and political structures were all in flux.[42]

It is hardly surprising that in this social climate, organized violence, crucial to initiating the changes in the first place, above all through collectivization, acquired an increasingly salient role. Systematic coercion, the third main feature of the Stalinist counter-revolution, involved an enormous enhancement in the powers of the secret police (the GPU, later the NKVD), responsible for, *inter alia*, the system of labour camps. Perhaps some five million slave labourers toiled in the Gulag Archipelago at the end of the 1930s.[43] The camp population, formed by waves of political dissenters and then by kulaks and *podkulachniki* in the early 1930s, was, of course, swelled by the victims of the Great Terror of 1936–8. These purges, in which several hundred thousand people perished, were, however, directed primarily at Bolshevik Party activists.[44] Those who escaped these very direct forms of state violence were subject to other kinds of coercion. A series of increasingly repressive labour laws were adopted, culminating in a decree of June 1940 which made job-changing and truancy criminal offences.[45] In 1933–4, two old Tsarist practices – internal passports and the *propiska*, or system of compulsory registration with the police – were reintroduced.

Coercion alone, however, is not enough to explain the regime's successful transformation of Russian society. Although the mass of workers and peasants were victims of the 'Stalin revolution', a minority of the population benefited from the changes it wrought. The social mobility unleashed by these changes is the fourth aspect essential to understanding the counter-revolution. Western scholars have recently tended to lay great stress on the extent to which the years 1927–31 saw a 'Cultural Revolution' in the USSR. The late NEP period was a time of growing social tensions in the cities, reflecting the rising level of unemployment and the evident contrast between the condition of the mass of the urban population and that of the 'NEP bourgeoisie' prospering from the revival of private enterprise after 1921. To a minority, particularly of young party activists, the abrupt shift in policy in 1928–9 marked a welcome end to this situation and an opportunity to participate in the heroic task of constructing 'socialism'. They were rallied to this task by various initiatives on the part of the regime. First, a rhetoric of acute class war was adopted and various Utopian visions of instant change in different areas of social life (culture, law, and urban planning, for example) were promoted; common to all was a voluntarism summed up by the slogan 'There is no fortress which Bolsheviks cannot storm.' Secondly, an assault was mounted on the old, predominantly non-Communist intelligentsia which previously had been tolerated and even favoured because of its possession of scarce skills. This shift in policy was announced by the Shakhty trial of May–June 1928 and followed by mass arrests of engineers and the 'social purging' of the state apparatus. Finally, the Komsomol (Young Communist League) was mobilized *en masse* to drive the peasants into collective farms.[46]

This 'Cultural Revolution' is sometimes used by historians to support the claim that the First Five-Year Plan consummated the social transformations unleashed by October 1917.[47] But this interpretation vastly underestimates the differences between the 1917 Revolution and its putative successor at the end of the 1920s. For one thing, the 'Cultural Revolution' was largely directed, indeed manipulated, from above. But, more fundamentally, the social meaning of the changes involved was upward mobility for a minority at a time when the mass of the population was experiencing an appalling decline in its material conditions. Rapid industrialization demanded that unskilled workers became skilled, that skilled workers became foremen, that technicians became engineers. Apprenticeship schools were massively expanded to provide workers with a secondary education and thereby to meet industry's demand for better trained personnel. The consequence was a large-scale influx of workers and ex-workers into managerial and technical positions. The main conditions of access to the numbers of these *vydvizhentsy* (promotees) were party membership and technical training. Between 1930 and 1933 some 660,000 'worker-Communists', amounting to between ten and fifteen per cent of the industrial workforce in 1930, moved into white-collar positions. This considerable social mobility did not alter the fact that the class structure of Soviet society was crystallizing around the intensive exploitation of the mass of workers and peasants. Nevertheless, the rise of some workers out of their class and the privileges granted others – the shock-workers and Stakhanovites rewarded for high productivity – helped to widen the regime's social base.[48]

The enthusiasms unleashed by the 'Cultural Revolution', combined with the more general flux characteristic of the First Five-Year Plan era, were socially destabilizing. Hence what Nicholas S. Timasheff called the 'Great Retreat' of the early and mid-1930s.[49] The voluntarist, class-war rhetoric was replaced by more conservative policies. First, the regime explicitly adopted a policy of encouraging wider pay differentials and more generally granting material privileges to specialists and managers: this shift was marked by Stalin's famous 1931 attack on 'egalitarianism' as having 'nothing in common with Marxian Socialism'.[50] Growing inequalities had in fact been a feature of Russian society since the mid-1920s. Stalin's speech explicitly legitimized divisions which already existed. The widening of differentials was indeed part of the more general post-1929 policy of, in Lewin's words, 'promoting a more powerful class of bosses – the *nachal'stvo*, composed of top managers in the enterprises and top administrators in state agencies'. He argues that '[t]he creation of a hierarchical scaffolding of dedicated bosses, held together by discipline, privilege and power, was a deliberate strategy of social engineering to help stabilize the flux'. The position of the factory director in particular was enhanced: 'endowed with quasi-police power in the workplace', his role was summed up by the injunction of Stalin's prize bully Kaganovich that 'the earth should tremble when the director walks round the plant'.[51] A third element in the regime's efforts to 'stabilize the flux' consisted in concessions to the peasantry: in particular, the formal recognition of collective farm members' right to sell grain on the free market and to a private plot and a cow. At the same time peasants' mobility was limited by the denial to them of internal passports. A tributary relationship between the state and the peasantry was thus established. Finally, the regime increasingly appealed to the traditional organic unities of nation and family, a shift reflected in the repeal of many of the major social reforms achieved by the October Revolution: thus divorce was made much more difficult in 1935 and abortion banned the following year.

The 'Great Retreat' did not prevent the convulsive burst of violence that decimated the ruling party itself in the late 1930s. Recent research, notably by J. Arch Getty, has encouraged the interpretation of the Terror as a social process rather than, as traditionally believed, the expression of the malign personality of the despot himself. Getty draws attention to the conflicts within the bureaucracy – between 'radicals' such as Molotov and 'conservatives' such as Ordzhonikidze over the pace of economic growth, and between the party centre and the regional secretaries who constantly ignored its injunctions. Stalin's role on this analysis was less that of omnipotent tyrant than of a broker manoeuvring between different factions. In 1936–7, however, he swung his weight behind the 'radicals' pressing for an all-out offensive against their opponents. The chief instrument of this policy was Yezhov, a 'cultural revolutionary' placed in charge of the NKVD in September 1936. The Terror thus unleashed involved, as well as the show trials which wiped out most of the surviving leaders of the October Revolution, the elimination of those in the economic apparatus denounced by Molotov as 'limiters' and 'underestimators', and of the local leaderships, whom the party rank-and-file were cynically encouraged to criticize and remove. Mass arrests of party officials in the summer and autumn of 1937 left not one regional secretary in place at the end of the year. The Yezhovschina was thus a last bout of 'Cultural Revolution', which like its Chinese successor in the late 1960s involved mass mobilizations around anti-bureaucratic rhetoric in order to settle disputes within the ruling class.[52]

Whatever the precise mechanics of the Terror, its social consequences are not in doubt. The Yezhovschina completed the process of upward mobility begun under the First Five-Year Plan. Sheila Fitzpatrick observes:

The careers of Aleksei Kosygin and Dimitri Ustinov [respectively Prime Minister and Defence Minister under Brezhnev] . . . – both working-class *vydvizhentsy* of the First Five-Year Plan period, graduating respectively in 1935 and 1934, and by 1941 holding ministerial positions in the government of the USSR – exemplify, if in extreme form, the dizzying rise of thousands. The First Five-Year Plan *vydvizhentsy* are, in fact, the 'Brezhnev generation' – the core of the sub-Politburo elite in the forties under Stalin, and of the top political leadership of the fifties and sixties.[53]

The Terror can thus be seen as the political consolidation of the counter-revolution. The slaughter wiped out the generation of Bolsheviks who had been shaped by the underground struggle against Tsarism and led the October Revolution itself. All the different factions in the battles of the 1920s – Trotskyists, Zinovievites, Bukharinites, Stalinists, even perpetrators of the Terror such as Yezhov himself – were swept away. Their shoes were filled by the *vydvizhentsy* who had risen thanks to the upheavals after 1928. The 'thaw' which followed Stalin's death in 1953 and Khrushchev's 1956 secret speech above all guaranteed that this generation would not itself succumb to a new instalment of the Yezhovschina. The new men advanced by the 'Stalin revolution' were to dominate Soviet politics until Gorbachev's accession to the General Secretaryship in 1985.[54] No connections with the revolutionary past inhibited the Brezhnev generation from fully identifying with the Stalinist system as it emerged from the turmoil of the 1930s.

Whatever contribution the original revolutionary period may have made to shaping that system (a question to which I return in chapter 4 below), the historical record leaves little doubt of the qualitative difference between Bolshevism and Stalinism. As a result of the transformations of the 1930s, Lewin argues, '[t]he party became an organization of an unprecedented type: a bureaucratic-political administration, highly centralized and geared to mobilization, regimentation, and control, entirely different from what it had been under Lenin.'[55] Articulated on to this political structure was the bureaucratic command economy as it had emerged from the First and Second Five-Year Plans (1928–37). Under the system which evolved during the 1930s, each individual enterprise was given a specific output target in the annual plan formulated by the State Planning Commission (Gosplan) through a process of bargaining involving central planners, the industrial ministries responsible for different sectors, and the enterprise directors themselves. Economic co-ordination took an extremely hierarchical form: the targets drawn up by Gosplan were legally binding on the enterprises. Moreover, not simply were output targets set by the centre, but supplies were allocated centrally. Access to inputs depended on the distribution of certificates by Gosplan and Gossnab (the State Committee on Material-Technical Supplies).[56]

Stalinism, this system in which social power was concentrated in the hands of the central political bureaucracy at the top of the party-state apparatus, survived for some sixty years, from the First Five-Year Plan to the crisis at the end of the 1980s. It is, as Cliff argues, best seen as a variant of capitalism, bureaucratic state capitalism. Marx ascribed two main defining features to the capitalist mode of production – the separation of labour-power from the means of production and its transformation into a commodity which the worker must sell in order to live, and the accumulation of surplus-value, its reinvestment in further production forced on individual capitals by their competitive struggle with one another.[57] Both these features took shape in the USSR under the First Five-Year Plan. In many respects the collectivization of agriculture bears a close analogy with the expropriation of the English peasantry which Marx analysed in Part Eight of *Capital* Volume I, on the 'primitive accumulation' of capital. In both cases the direct producers were deprived of their land and therefore reduced to a condition where many had no choice but to become labourers in the new industries. But the workers were not thereby transformed into slaves of the Stalinist state. One of the most striking aspects of working-class resistance during the 1930s was the very high levels of labour turnover: the average industrial worker changed jobs every eight months in 1930 and every 13 months in 1939.[58]

The ability of workers to move from enterprise to enterprise created a labour market in which relative wages varied as directors sought to attract and retain employees through pay incentives. Alec Nove's description of these wage variations, a consequence of the fact that '[m]inistries and enterprises in practice compete for labour', highlights processes already at work under the First Five-Year Plan:

> In this situation, market forces (i.e. supply of and demand for different kinds of labour) affect relative incomes in two ways. First, *they affect the decisions of government*. Thus, if at a given wage-rate there are not enough instrument mechanics, carpenters, miners, computer operators, or anyone willing to work north of the Arctic Circle, then the official income scales can be (and often are) altered to ensure a supply response. Secondly, since official scales are seldom altered and may not fit the local situation, managers try to find ways of *evading the official scales*.[59]

Capitalism involves, however, more than the transformation of labour-power into a commodity. The period of the First and Second Five-Year Plans saw a drastic rearrangement of economic priorities. The share of consumer goods in total output fell from 67.2 per cent in 1927–8 to 39.0 per cent in 1940; over the same period the share of producer goods rose from 32.8 per cent to 61.0 per cent.[60] These figures imply the systematic subordination of consumption to investment in heavy industry. Indeed, as we saw above, this very high rate of accumulation depended on a dramatic increase in the rate of surplus-extraction from the working class. As Cliff argues,

> A quick accumulation of capital on the basis of a low level of production, of a small national income per capita, must put a burdensome pressure on the consumption of the masses, on their standard of living. Under such conditions, the bureaucracy, transformed into a personification of capital, for whom the accumulation of capital is the be-all and end-all here, must get rid of all remnants of workers' control, must substitute conviction in the labour-process by coercion, must atomize the working class, must force all social-political life into a totalitarian mould.[61]

The main mechanism which Marx analysed as impelling capitals to accumulate was their competitive interaction on the market. But the First Five-Year Plan involved the large-scale suppression of the internal market, while foreign trade, though important as a source of Western technology, played only a limited role in shaping the overall pattern of economic development of the USSR. The mechanism enforcing accumulation on the Stalin regime was competition of a different sort. It was, as we saw, the fear of war with more advanced powers which underlay the decision to industrialize in the first instance. Military rivalry – with Britain in the late 1920s, with Germany between 1933 and 1945, with the US and its allies after 1945 – imposed on the USSR a set of priorities favouring above all investment in defence-related heavy industry. This pattern persisted into the era of *perestroika*. The economist Selyunin wrote in 1988:

> The consumption fund accounts for 60 per cent of income and the savings fund for 40 per cent. Such a high composition of savings is, essentially, a wartime standard.
>
> The shift toward the manufacture of producer goods has put us in the paradoxical situation where accelerated rates of development and more rapid growth in national income have very little effect on the standard of living. The economy is working more and more for itself, rather than for man.[62]

Production for production's sake was, of course, what Marx believed to be the defining feature of capitalism. When this pattern first emerged in the USSR at the beginning of the 1930s it was far from exceptional. The Great Depression led to a general fragmentation of the world market into rival trade blocs, as each major power carved out its own economic zone protected ultimately by its military strength. This trend to autarky was accompanied by a qualitative leap in state direction of the domestic economy. Outside Russia the most extreme case was Nazi Germany, where the restoration of full employment was made possible by rearmament and accompanied by an extension of the state sector (for example, the vast Hermann Göring works) and increased government direction of private firms through such mechanisms as exchange-control and the Four-Year Plan. Elsewhere the tendency towards autarkic state capitalism was less pronounced but evident all the same: Roosevelt's New Deal in the US and the National Government's programme of cartellization and nationalization in Britain demonstrate its existence even in the liberal democracies. The Stalin counter-revolution was thus not the perfection of a rival social system but the furthest point reached by a universal tendency towards militarized state capitalism.[63] One main source, however, of the crisis which struck the USSR in the 1980s was the fact that the pattern of development which had placed it in the vanguard of capitalism in the 1930s now condemned it to increasing obsolescence.

2.2   THE CONTRADICTIONS OF AUTHORITARIAN REFORM

The moment of death can also be the moment of truth for a social system. When the system is at the point of disintegration, its fundamental features are thrown into sharp relief. Such has been the fate of the Stalinist regimes. Their progressive collapse in the late 1980s refuted most of the established analyses of 'really existing socialism'. This is true of the two main theories favoured by the Western left. One is Trotsky's interpretation of the Stalin regime as a 'degenerated workers' state', whose original insights were progressively obscured by the dogmatic efforts of his orthodox successors to extend it to the 'socialist' states of Eastern Europe and the Third World. The best-known contemporary proponent of orthodox Trotskyism is Ernest Mandel, who argued as recently as 1980, on the basis of the performance of the Stalinist states during the world recession of 1974–5, that:

Once again, history has confirmed that an economy based on collective ownership of the major means of production, central planning, and a state monopoly of foreign trade is qualitatively superior to a capitalist market economy in its ability to avert great cyclical fluctuations, over-production crises, and unemployment, despite the monstrous waste and imbalances caused by the bureaucratic monopoly of economic and political management and regardless of the distance that still separates them from a genuine socialist economy.[64]

The picture of the Soviet economy when Mandel was writing painted by Gorbachev's adviser Abel Aganbegyan hardly encourages us to view it as a social system more advanced than Western capitalism: 'In the period 1981–85 there was practically no economic growth. Unprecedented stagnation and crisis occurred during the period 1979–82, when production of 40 per cent of all industrial goods actually fell.'[65] Indeed, as evidence of waste and inefficiency in the USSR has accumulated in the past two decades, the left, West and East alike, have increasingly been inclined to view Stalinism as a form of society qualitatively *inferior* to capitalism. The original version of this idea was the theory, formulated by Max Shachtman and other dissident followers of Trotsky during the Second World War, that 'bureaucratic collectivism', a new form of class society, prevailed in the USSR.[66] But in the 1970s and 1980s variations on this theme were increasingly widely heard on the Western left (in the English-speaking world an analysis of this sort was promoted especially by Hillel Ticktin and the journal *Critique*) and among dissident socialists in the East itself (Rudolph Bahro, János Kis, and Boris Kagarlitsky, for example). The idea of a post-capitalist class society has always been ambiguous in the sense that it left open whether such a society was more or less progressive than capitalism, but the experience of the past twenty years has led its proponents strongly to argue for the inferiority of the Stalinist regimes to the West.

At their most extreme such analyses resemble what is probably still the hegemonic interpretation of Stalinism in the liberal democracies, that of totalitarianism, according to which the USSR and its like are closed societies so pervasively and rigidly controlled from above as to be unamenable to any kind of internally generated change. Thus, in an essay first published in 1985, Ferenc Fehér and Agnes Heller asserted of Eastern Europe that 'the hope for radical change is gone in the region, at least for the foreseeable future'. The ultimate reason why a 'complete detotalization of East European states is an excluded possibility' was apparently the political passivity of the peoples of the

USSR itself: 'Stalin's long and efficient training wiped out the spirit of rebellion from a populace which assesses its social conditions more realistically than do Western observers.' These and many other dogmatic utterances by Fehér and Heller were, happily, soon refuted when an effervescent welter of social, political, and cultural movements appeared in the USSR under *glasnost*, followed by the great popular risings in Eastern Europe. The absurdity of the entire line of thinking taken to such extremes by Fehér and Heller is indicated by their pronouncement, in the course of an attack on the Western peace movement that could have been written in the US State Department, that '[t]here is no way to convince the populace of any under-industrialized area of any Soviet society which lacks elementary industrial goods and other social amenities, often even electricity, that a nuclear plant could have dangerous side effects'.[67] These lines were republished the year after the Chernobyl disaster. Even if the claim made by the *Financial Times* that 'the East German revolution was perhaps the first in history in which dissatisfaction about industrial pollution played an important role' involved some hyperbole, ecological issues proved to be one of the most effective bases of mass mobilization by the democratic movements in the USSR and Eastern Europe alike.[68]

More fundamental, however, than any specific errors of prediction is the failure of attempts to theorize the Stalinist regimes as a social system different from and inferior to Western capitalism to account for the crisis which afflicted these states in the 1980s. For the causes of this crisis were in large part rooted in Stalinism's historic *success*. Let us, in the first instance, recall the target set by Stalin for the USSR in 1931, to 'make good' Russia's distance behind the 'advanced countries . . . in ten years'. Although this target had not been met by 1941, the heavy industry built up during the first two Five-Year Plans (1928–37) provided the economic base of the USSR's war effort against Nazi Germany. By the 1950s the Soviet Union had become the second largest industrial economy in the world. Soviet industrial output per head was 25 per cent of the West European average in 1929, 84 per cent in 1963. The methods used to achieve this transformation – centralized allocation of resources within a largely closed, state-controlled economy – did not differ qualitatively from the response of the Western powers to the economic slump of the 1930s, and were indeed adopted largely in response to the pressure of military competition from the more advanced economies.[69] The East European states, subjected to Soviet political and military hegemony and transformed along Stalinist lines in the late 1940s, initially enjoyed a comparable breakthrough. M. C. Kaser writes:

> The average rate of growth achieved in the region during the first two
> decades of central planning (1950–70) was better than the peak rates
> shown in the best interwar years (1925–29). The two least developed
> countries grew as fast as the two fastest growing countries in the best
> interwar five-year period, Czechoslovakia and Hungary.[70]

The dynamism of the Eastern bloc in the late 1950s led senior
American officials such as CIA Director Allen Dulles to appear before
Congress warning of 'the Soviet economic-technological challenge'.[71]

Yet in the 1960s the picture began to change. Soviet growth rates
began to slip around the middle of that decade. The average growth
rate during the 1970s, 2.6 per cent, was comparable to those of West
European economies afflicted by the two great world recessions of
those years, but well below plan targets.[72] By the 1980s, the Soviet
economy was, according to Aganbegyan, stagnating. Some East
European states, notably Poland, were experiencing even more acute
crises. What were the sources of this predicament? To some degree, it
reflected the maturing of the Stalinist economies. The fast growth
rates sustained before the 1960s and 1970s were an achievement of
'extensive industrialization', in which new plant was constructed and
set to work using the plentiful reserves of cheap labour and raw
materials available especially in the USSR itself. It became a commonplace of Eastern reformers and Western analysts from the 1960s
onwards that, as these reserves dried up, further growth depended on
a shift to an 'intensive' model in which output was increased through
higher productivity and more rapid technological innovation. It
became as much a commonplace to argue that the bureaucratic
command economy erected in the 1930s represented a major obstacle
to effecting such a transformation.[73]

Attention increasingly focused on the pathologies of this kind of
economy – the apparently endemic shortages of both consumer and
capital goods, the waste occasioned by investment cycles usually
culminating in many projects being left unfinished, the inefficiencies
involved in poor co-ordination between sectors and the planners'
inability to process the vast amount of information accumulated at
the centre. The Hungarian economist János Kornai has made one of
the most rigorous attempts to theorize these phenomena. He argues
that these involve the '[c]onstant reproduction of shortage', caused by
the fact that 'there is no *self-imposed* limit to the demand for
investment resources', so that firms tend to hoard inputs, and thus

create shortages, which sets to work a vicious circle in which the
scarcity of goods leads to a more intense 'quantity drive' by industry,
in turn intensifying shortages.[74] But Kornai does not satisfactorily
explain the sources of what he calls this 'almost insatiable investment
hunger'. Martin Wolf makes a suggestive comparison:

> One way of thinking about the abnormality of the Soviet economy is
> that it is an extreme kind of war economy. More is involved than the
> burden of expenditure on defence. Also significant is the focus on
> heavy industry and indifference to consumption; the economy's isola-
> tion and extreme centralization; the repressed inflation; the appeals to
> collective sacrifice; and the paranoia.[75]

Indeed, the phenomena of shortage and waste analysed by Kornai
were pervasive features of the war economies organized by all the
powers in 1914–18 (when they broke the back of the Tsarist regime)
and 1939–45. The long era of military competition between the USSR
and the advanced economies, which began in the late 1920s and was
continued by the Cold War, locked the Soviet economy into an
organizational structure that bred the inefficiencies diagnosed by
Kornai and others. The economic priority given the military must of
itself help explain the growth slowdown which set in during the
1960s. On one recent Soviet estimate, the total gross domestic
product (GDP) of the USSR was about half that of the US in 1987;
Soviet GDP per head was only 42 per cent of that of the US. The
burden imposed on the USSR of matching the military expenditure of
a far larger and more advanced economy has been enormous. Around
13 per cent of Soviet GDP was spent on defence in 1987, twice the
American figure.[76] Investible resources which could have been devoted to improving the productivity of civilian industries were instead
diverted into the development of ever more costly and sophisticated
weapons-systems.

More fundamental still to explaining the crisis of Stalinism has
been the transformation of the world economy over the past generation. Particularly since the end of the long boom of the 1960s and
1970s, the most important trend has been towards the globalization
of capital. Trade and investment have become increasingly interna-
tionalized with the development of what Nigel Harris called a 'global
manufacturing system' in which large increases in productivity could
be realized by organizing production across national borders. The
increasing salience of the multinational corporation as a form of
productive organization was matched by the development of enor-

mous international flows of financial investment, as the banking and securities industries also broke national barriers. This global integration of capital implied a considerable reduction in the economic power of the nation-state. State intervention in the economy did not cease – witness the use of Keynesian policies of demand stimulation and credit expansion by New Right governments in the US and Britain during the 1980s – but it no longer involved the kind of centralized resource-allocation pervasive in the advanced countries as well as the USSR between the 1930s and 1950s.[77]

The globalization of capital left the Stalinist states stranded. The forms of organization which had transformed the Soviet Union into a superpower and industrialized Eastern Europe no longer corresponded to world-wide patterns of development. The economic miracle of the 1970s and 1980s was the industrialization of parts of the Third World. Typically these newly industrializing countries (NICs) were able to break out of the old cycle of underdevelopment thanks to the role played by a highly interventionist state. Thus the South Korean state controlled two-thirds of national investment and directed the investment decisions of the *chaebol*, the fifty giant private companies. M. K. Datta-Chaudhuri commented: 'No state, outside the socialist bloc, ever came anywhere near to this measure of control over the economy's investible resources.'[78] This state-directed accumulation was not, however, oriented towards building a national economy as far as possible independent of the rest of the world. Rather, it was intended to break into world markets – in textiles and garments in the 1960s, in steel and shipbuilding in the 1970s, in vehicles and consumer electronics in the 1980s. The most successful NICs, those on the Pacific Rim, triumphed as exporters of manufactured goods.

The obsolescence of the bureaucratic state-capitalist model erected in the USSR in the 1930s and transplanted to Eastern Europe after the war became increasingly evident. Poland's crisis was especially acute, since its rulers sought in the 1970s to alleviate internal social tensions by a dash for growth – financing large-scale investments by borrowing heavily from Western banks in the hope that these loans would be repaid with foreign exchange earned by exporting much of the output of the new plant. The onset of a second major world recession at the end of the 1970s destroyed these plans and left Poland in the grips of a debt crisis very similar to that of the Latin American NICs – Brazil, Mexico, and Argentina.[79] The plight of the USSR itself was masked by the fact that the surge in oil prices during the 1970s allowed the Brezhnev regime to import Western technology and consumer goods and thereby to put off the day of economic reckoning. But as the 1980s dawned the difficulties faced by the Soviet Union became increasingly evident. Its lack of integration in the world market denied the USSR access to the kind of increases in labour productivity contingent on participation in an international division of labour; its dependence on imported technology placed the Soviet Union under increasing pressure as the arms race accelerated by the revival of Cold War in the late 1970s encouraged the development of ever more sophisticated weapons-systems and as the fall in the price of oil highlighted its reliance on raw-material exports vulnerable to the fluctuations of world markets.

What Chris Harman calls the 'shift from national capitalism to multinational capitalism' at a global level thus created powerful external forces threatening the USSR with stagnation, even collapse, unless its closed economy were somehow broken open.[80] But at the same time internal pressures for change built up, particularly during Brezhnev's General Secretaryship (1964–82). Boris Kagarlitsky argues:

> The Brezhnev era is usually viewed by Western observers as a time of political standstill and economic stagnation ... But in saying this we are telling only half the truth. The 1970s were a period of major social and socio-psychological shifts which will have far-reaching consequences for Soviet history. The processes which have occurred can only be compared in their significance with the social changes which occurred in Russia at the time of the 'tranquil' reign of Alexander III [1881–94] and which prefigured the 1905 Revolution ... In the 1970s an industrial society was definitely formed in our country, the process of urbanization was completed and a new generation grew up, shaped by the conditions of Europeanized city life.[81]

The urbanization of the USSR in the past generation has been spectacular. In 1960 the urban population was still only 49 per cent of the total: by 1985 it had risen to 65 per cent (70 per cent in the Russian Federation). As significant as this overall trend was what Moshe Lewin calls 'an internal regrouping of the inhabitants in favour of the biggest agglomerations'. The 272 Soviet cities with more than 100,000 inhabitants in 1980 accounted for a third of the total population. The number of cities with over a million inhabitants rose from three in 1959 to twenty-three in 1980.[82] These changes were accompanied by a significant increase in living standards. Jerry Hough observes:

The Brezhnev era in particular was the one in which the Soviet Union became an appliance society, in which people moved from a one-room apartment to a one-bedroom apartment, and in which meat consumption (despite a temporary plateau in the late 1970s) moved towards British levels.

Between 1960 and 1985 the kilograms of meat consumed per capita rose from 39.5 to 62.4, the square metres of urban living space per capita from 8.9 to 14.3, and the percentages of families with fridges from 4 to 92, washing machines from 4 to 70, and television sets from 8 to 99.[83] Finally, the social structure of the urban population became more differentiated and complex. The manual working class became an increasingly stable, self-reproducing group, no longer recruited primarily from peasant immigrants and possessing rising levels of skill and education. As in the West, its expansion was outpaced by that of the broad and ambiguous category of 'employees' embracing both routine white-collar workers and an 'intelligentsia' composed of highly-educated professionals, managers and administrators.[84]

These socio-economic changes were held up by the Brezhnev leadership and its apologists as a sign that the USSR had arrived at 'mature' or 'developed socialism' (a category which had, among other things, the advantage of delaying the transition to communism till the Greek kalends). In fact, they increased the regime's problems. Rising levels of education and consumption raised expectations that were not fulfilled. The intelligentsia chafed under the restraints imposed by bureaucratic structures whose dysfunctions were evident to all and resented the relatively narrow income inequalities which left them poorly off by comparison with their Western counterpart, the 'new middle class'. Workers too complained about low living standards, incompetent management, and oppressive work relations. Cultural changes made possible by the expansion of secondary and higher education and the development of an urban consumer society created a literate and sophisticated population impatient with the lies, distortions, and platitudes served up by the official media. Kagarlitsky cites a Soviet sociologist who argued that 'the cultural level of the masses became on average somewhat higher during the 1970s than the cultural level of the ruling elite'.[85] Workers, managers, and professionals alike nurtured a strong sense of social injustice promoted by widespread knowledge of the immense material privileges possessed especially by those in the upper echelons of the *nomenklatura*.[86] Greater contact with the West contributed to the growing awareness that 'mature socialism' was lagging behind its supposedly inferior competitors and helped to stimulate the development of an unofficial culture in which rock music played a large part. By the time of Brezhnev's death in November 1982 the state ideology had been hollowed out as large sections of the population began openly to opt for alternatives ranging from the new youth culture to traditionalist Russian nationalism, the latter tacitly encouraged by one wing of the bureaucracy. The USSR entered during the 1980s into a profound crisis of hegemony.

The USSR's authoritarian modernization had run up against its limits. The organizational forms which had made possible rapid industrialization after 1928 now inhibited further development. At the same time, that very process of industrialization had created an urbanized and educated population no longer willing to put up with the inefficiencies and inequities of the Stalinist system. It was against this background that the conflicts within the bureaucracy between conservatives and reformers – intrinsic to Soviet political life since Stalin's death – became more acute.[87] The alignments of forces and processes which brought Gorbachev to the General Secretaryship remain obscure.[88] What is not in doubt, however, is that his policies represented an attempt to respond to the crisis of the Stalinist system by reforming rather than dismantling that system. Many on the Western left have argued that Gorbachev's programme is more radical. Thus, according to Tariq Ali, '[i]n order to preserve the Soviet Union, Gorbachev needs to complete the political revolution (which is already under way), but one based on an abolition of the whole *nomenklatura* system of privileges on which the power of the bureaucracy rests'.[89] In fact, *perestroika*, the restructuring of the Soviet economy and of political and social life more generally, initially took the form of marginal adjustments designed primarily to enhance and modernize central controls – Zhores Medvedev described Aganbegyan's project as 'a computerized version of the command economy' – accompanied by a powerful rhetoric of change and the encouragement of criticism under the slogan of *glasnost* (openness). Medvedev summed up Gorbachev's first two years by saying that the General Secretary was 'neither a liberal nor a bold reformer. He prefers modifications, administrative methods and economic adjustments to structural and political reforms'.[90] Gorbachev's boldest departure initially was in foreign policy, where he sought improved relations with the West in the hope of reducing the burden of defence spending.

The radicalization of Gorbachev's domestic policies, especially after his speech to the January 1987 plenum of the CPSU Central

Committee, might be taken to confute judgements such as Medvedev's. But the process through which the reformers within the apparatus moved towards much more far-reaching political and economic measures did not reflect any carefully worked-out strategy but rather the dynamics of the struggles under way within the bureaucracy itself. Even the relatively moderate reforms of Gorbachev's initial period in office were largely sabotaged by apparatchiks in the economic ministries. Gorbachev and his allies became convinced that only more radical measures could salvage the system – the partial dismantling of the command economy through the replacement of 'vertical' controls from the centre with 'horizontal' market mechanisms to co-ordinate enterprises and compel them to become more efficient, and the introduction of a large measure of political liberalization, especially in the form of competitive elections to party and state bodies. These political reforms – most notably the establishment of a new parliament, the Congress of People's Deputies, the elections to which in March 1989 were the first genuinely contested since the aftermath of the October Revolution – involved an appeal by the reformers for popular support in their struggle against the conservatives. This step, the decision to take the differences within the apparatus to a larger audience, marked the real turning point in the process of *glasnost*, the moment at which the revolutionary overthrow of the Stalinist regimes became a real possibility.

Gorbachev's programme, remained, even after its radicalization in 1986–7, one of authoritarian reform, an attempt to preserve the Stalinist system by modernizing it from above. There is, of course, nothing new about such strategies: they have been frequently attempted in the past two centuries of world history, and indeed date back even further in Russia, to the time of Peter the Great. But authoritarian reformers are vulnerable to a contradiction diagnosed by Tocqueville when he wrote: 'The most perilous moment for a bad government is one when it seeks to mend its ways.'[91] The dilemma confronting the reforming regime is that the changes it attempts are likely to be too radical for many of its own supporters but too moderate for the mass of the population. The resulting paralysis of an internally divided ruling class creates the conditions in which a popular revolution from below can take place. Tocqueville after all based his analysis on the experience of the Great French Revolution, which began as an attempt by the absolute monarchy of Louis XVI to reform itself and was unleashed by the consequent polarization between aristocratic reaction and popular radicalization. Chris

Harman detected a similar dynamic at work in the various attempts to reform the Stalinist regimes in the 1950s and 1960s:

> In order to try to overcome conservative sections of the bureaucracy opposing reforms in the 1950s, the central political apparatus (or a section of it) attempt to mobilize other elements in the bureaucracy. This was the real significance of the anti-Stalin campaigns of 1953, 1956 and 1962. But there were clear limits within which this was possible. Much of the conservative resistance could not be overcome without the danger arising of the repressive apparatus vis-à-vis the rest of society being paralysed, thus unleashing forces that might easily turn against the bureaucracy as a whole (as in East Germany in 1953, in Poland and Hungary in 1956, in Czechoslovakia in 1968–9, and in China in 1966–7). In Russia itself the bureaucracy stopped short of taking measures that might have had such disastrous effects from its point of view.[92]

In the late 1980s, faced with a far more profound economic and social crisis than had confronted the rulers of the USSR after Stalin's death, Gorbachev and his fellow reformers decided to risk such 'disastrous effects' by appealing to the masses. They opened Pandora's box, freeing an effervescent throng of political forces that threatened the very existence of the Stalinist system – the Popular Fronts demanding radical democratic change, the nationalist movements in the various non-Russian republics, notably in the Prebaltic and Transcaucasia, pressing increasingly for independence from the USSR, and workers' organizations formed outside the official unions, especially after the miners' strikes in the summer and autumn of 1989. This process of political radicalization helped in turn to stimulate popular movements in Eastern Europe rewarded in the winter of 1989 with the collapse of the Stalinist regimes there. Reform had accelerated to revolution. But what did these changes portend?

2.3   POLITICAL OR SOCIAL REVOLUTION?

Writing just before the upheavals of 1989 Tim Garton Ash described the process under way as 'refolution', 'a singular mixture of both reform and revolution' marked by 'a strong and essential element of voluntary, deliberate reform by an enlightened minority (but only a minority) in the still ruling Communist Parties' involving crucially 'an unprecedented retreat: undertaking to share power, and even – *mirabile dictu* – talk of giving it up altogether if they lose an election'.[93] Ash had in mind the round-table negotiations between the regime and the opposition in Poland and Hungary. But change when it came in Eastern Europe proved to be not a gradual process carefully controlled from the top but a series of abrupt transformations powered by popular rebellion against bureaucratic rule. Reform from above and mass mobilization from below interacted to bring about, quite unexpectedly, and with extraordinary rapidity, the abandonment of their monopoly of power by the Stalinist parties and their replacement by governments pledged to the introduction of liberal parliamentary regimes. The upheavals in Eastern Europe are a remarkable instance of the role of unintended consequences in history: the effects of the 'enlightened minority' of reformers in the Stalinist regimes far outreached their intentions. This outcome helped to push Gorbachev and his allies into an increasingly conservative stance, in which *glasnost* was replaced by a recharged authoritarianism.

If we follow Perry Anderson in defining revolution as 'an episode of convulsive political transformation, compressed in time and concentrated in target, that has a determinate beginning – when the old state apparatus is still intact – and a finite end, when that apparatus is decisively ended and a new one erected in its stead', then we can, provisionally at least, describe the upheavals in Eastern Europe as revolutions.[94] One form of political regime – Stalinist one-party rule – was being supplanted under popular pressure by another – liberal democracy. But what was the social meaning of this political transformation? The most typical interpretation, on the left as well as the right, was that the overthrow of Stalinism in Eastern Europe would lead to the restoration of capitalism. Thus *New Left Review*, while welcoming 'the transition to democracy', feared 'a capitalist restructuring of the East' and predicted the development of 'restorationist pressures'.[95]

Undoubtedly one of the most striking features of the new post-Stalinist governments in Eastern Europe was their commitment to what might best be described as Thatcherite economic policies – integration into the world market, privatization of state-owned industry, closure of inefficient plant, abolition of consumer subsidies – justified by appeal to the ideology of the Western New Right. Hayek and Friedman, the apostles of a return to *laissez faire*, proved to be the main inspiration of the economists infesting the new governments. Neo-liberal nostrums, and in particular the idea that the market is a necessary condition of both political freedom and economic efficiency, were swallowed whole by the opposition intellectuals brought to power by the revolutions. The ex-Marxist dissidents leading the Association of Free Democrats in Hungary, for example, yielded to no-one in their enthusiasm for the market. Acceptance of the market took a variety of forms. Take the case of Václav Havel, described by Tim Garton Ash as 'the outstanding literary-philosophical analyst of the Central European experience under communism' (though Ash did admit to finding 'something slightly worrying in . . . the virtual cult of personality' of which his own description of Havel is an instance).[96] Inspection of Havel's writing reveals him in fact to be philosophically a rather conventional romantic neo-conservative, with views akin to those of Prince Charles and the later Heidegger. Thus: 'We must honour with the humility of the wise the bounds of that natural world and the mystery which lies beyond them, admitting that there is something in the order of Being which evidently lies beyond them.' The 'anti-political politics' Havel derived from this philosophical orientation led him to dismiss 'the question about socialism and capitalism' as 'emerging from the depths of the last century'. This evasion didn't stop him ultimately from opting for the market: 'If we can defend our humanity, then perhaps there is a hope of sorts that we can also find some sort of more meaningful way of balancing our natural rights to participate in economic decision-making and to a dignified social status, with the tried driving force of all work: human enterprise realized in authentic market transactions.'[97]

What Neal Ascherson briskly dismisses as the 'muzziness' of 'anti-politics', the claim by the East European opposition in the mid-1980s to have transcended the division between right and left, proved only to be a transitional stage between its earlier belief that the Stalinist states could gradually be reformed and its emergence as the neo-liberal undertaker and heir of these states in 1989, though vestiges survived, for example, in the efforts of Havel and his associates in Civic Forum to blunt the impact of Czechoslovakia's subjection to market disciplines.[98] The Thatcherite economic programme which represented the new governments' attempt to subordinate their economies to 'the tried driving force of all work' implied, however, reductions in employment and living standards which, if achieved, would throw into the shade the achievements of New Right administrations in the West. While Czechoslovakia's 'velvet revolution' was still under way in November 1989, the *Financial Times* reported that 'Czechs turn to economists for deliverance', noting the popularity of neo-liberal economists such as Valtr Komarek, Václav Klaus, and Miloš Zeman. There was something ghoulish about the good humour with which these 'experts' at the threshold of power (Komarek became First Deputy Prime Minister and Klaus Finance Minister in the new government) promised economic austerity as the reward for political revolution. The *Financial Times* highlighted 'a common theme – the trading of democracy for a period of a fall in living standards – perhaps, Mr Zeman thinks, by 30 to 50 per cent. They bank not just upon an outpouring of democratic enthusiasm, but also a sense of national pride.'[99] Nor were the projections of an economic squeeze mere rhetoric. The subjection of the Polish economy in December 1989 to a 'shock cure' by Finance Minister Leszek Balcerowicz, involving a balanced budget and the abolition of price controls and subsidies, led to a 36 per cent reduction in real income in January 1990 alone.[100]

Were the pro-market policies of the post-Stalinist governments an aspect of the restoration of capitalism in Eastern Europe? To answer in the affirmative implied that some kind of post-capitalist social system had prevailed prior to the 1989 revolutions. But such an analysis was contradicted by the extraordinary ease with which Stalinism had been removed in Eastern Europe. Trotsky, for example, had argued that the restoration of capitalism in the USSR would require 'the intervention of military surgery':

> The Marxist thesis relating to the catastrophic character of the transfer of power from the hands of one class to another applies not only to revolutionary periods, when history sweeps madly ahead, but also to the periods of counterrevolution, when society rolls backwards. He who asserts that the Soviet government has been *gradually* changed from proletarian to bourgeois is only, so to speak, running backwards the film of reformism.[101]

Trotsky's use of the idea that the replacement of one social system by another is necessarily violent to argue that the USSR was still a degenerated workers' state under Stalin ignored the savagery involved in the transformations wrought after 1928 – Cliff describes the 1930s as a 'civil war of the bureaucracy against the masses, a civil war in which only one side was armed and organized'.[102] But the 1989 revolutions, abrupt and dramatic as they were, were remarkable for the absence of large-scale social conflict and violence. The confrontations between demonstrators and police in East Germany and Czechoslovakia involved a similar level of violence to the clashes between riot squads and striking miners in Mrs Thatcher's Britain. In Poland and Hungary even the factor of mass mobilization was absent: forty years of Stalinist rule, maintained by force against the workers' councils of Budapest in 1956 and against Solidarność in 1981, petered out in the round-table deals between the regimes and those whom they had long kept in prison. No doubt this had in part to do with the USSR's refusal to sanction the suppression of the democracy movements in Eastern Europe. As Tim Garton Ash observes, 'Romania was the exception that proves the rule. It is no accident that it was precisely in the state for so long most *in*dependent of Moscow that the resistance of the security arm of the powers-that-were was most fierce, bloody and prolonged'.[103]

But the replacement of the Brezhnev doctrine with the Sinatra doctrine ('I had it my way') – Soviet Foreign Ministry spokesman Gennady Gerasimov's way of describing how Gorbachev suddenly pulled the rug from under such faithful clients as Honecker and Jakeš – could not account for the enthusiasm with which large sections of the ruling *nomenklatura* greeted Eastern Europe's opening to the market. To understand this we must consider the nature of this group – what Jacek Kuroń and Karol Modzelewski called 'the central political bureaucracy'.[104] One study of the Soviet elite characterized it as numbering (in the early 1970s) some 227,000 persons in responsible or *nomenklatura* positions to which significant material privileges accrued – senior officials in the party, ministries, Komsomol, trade unions, military, police, and diplomatic service; key enterprise managers; and top intellectuals (academicians, heads of research institutes, editors, etc.).[105] Numerous other studies have established the extent to which the *nomenklatura* is a managerial organization: not only those working in the industrial ministries and running the enterprises but also in the party apparatus, notably the regional (*obkom*) secretaries, on whom considerable functions of economic co-ordination devolve, are chiefly concerned with the management of the economy.[106] The character of the central political bureaucracy in Eastern Europe was essentially the same.

The central role of the *nomenklatura* in economic management forced many of its members to face up to the increasing crisis of the bureaucratic model. Enterprise directors and regional secretaries were likely in any case to chafe under the restrictions imposed on them by the industrial ministries and central planners and to resent the endless hunt for workers and material inputs forced on them by endemic shortages. At the same time, the growing involvement of the East European economies in the world market – despite the slow pace of economic reform after the fall of Khrushchev and Dubček, Poland and Hungary in particular borrowed heavily in the West and sought to repay these loans by increasing hard-currency exports – acclimatized managers to co-operation with Western firms. Despite the Honecker regime's efforts to reduce trade with the West to avoid the kind of debt crisis experienced by Poland and Hungary in the 1980s, 30 per cent of East Germany's trade was with OECD countries on the eve of the revolution.[107] The need for advanced technology necessitated the encouragement of joint ventures with Western firms: by the middle of October 1989 there were 2,090 joint ventures registered in the USSR, Hungary, Poland, Czechoslovakia, Romania, and Bulgaria.[108] Experience both of the crisis of their own economies and of the advantages accruing from the internationalization of capital encouraged the most successful managers – for example, those running the *Kombinate*, the 126 vertically organized industrial combines dominating East Germany – to see their future as lying in the dismantling of the bureaucratic command system and greater integration with the Western multinationals.

Thus the *Financial Times* reported in January 1990:

> East Germany's giant state-owned monopolies will be transformed into joint stock companies with Eastern and Western shareholders if Mr Friedrich Wokurka, the Managing Director of Robotron, the country's largest electronic company, has anything to do with it . . . 'If international capital markets open up to the GDR then it will have to be equally open to them,' Mr Wokurka told the *Financial Times*. 'There can be no half measures.'

The interview continued with Wokurka, 'a party member, like nearly all managers of state enterprises', explaining that his

> enthusiasm for the market economy was not all that new . . . But until recently it was something he could voice only in the privacy of his own home. Like a number of other *Kombinate* directors, he saw red when reading articles by East German economists who advocated a 'third way' for the country – between socialism and capitalism.[109]

Wokurka was by no means exceptional. The opening of the Berlin Wall was followed by a flood of joint ventures agreed between West German multinationals and East German *Kombinate* – between both Volkswagen and Opel and IFA-Kombinat (cars), Pilz and Robotron (compact discs), Zeiss and VEB Jena (optics), among many others.[110]

Developments of this kind – more dramatic in East Germany because of its relatively advanced economy and imminent incorporation into the Federal Republic – were indicative of the limited character of the socio-economic changes under way in the East. Substantial sections of the old ruling class were abandoning the old autarkic mode of development for integration into international capital. Chris Harman describes this as 'moving sideways' – a shift from one variant of capitalism to another, from bureaucratic state capitalism to multinational capitalism.[111] This implied not so much the complete elimination of state capitalism – after all, state intervention remained a fundamental feature of the Western economies – but rather a process of social and economic restructuring which would allow much of the *nomenklatura* to transform itself from apparatchiks into private executives, either of locally owned firms or of the subsidiaries of Western multinationals.

The resulting reorganization would involve considerable changes in existing economic structures. An interview given to the *Financial Times* by Volkswagen chairman Carl Hahn implied that his joint venture with IFA-Kombinat would lead to the effective dismantling of the East German combine:

> At present, the East German auto industry is vertically integrated to a degree long since unheard of in the West. IFA-Kombinat includes everything from vehicle assembly to virtually the whole gamut of automotive components. 'This guarantees the highest degree of inefficiency,' says Mr Hahn.[112]

More generally, the efforts even by the most successful state capitalist economies to replicate within their borders all the industries required for autarkic development prevented them from reaping the benefits of the international division of labour. According to the *Financial Times*,

> Carl Zeiss Jena, one of the leading GDR high-tech companies, developed a one-megabit memory chip at a cost of Mark 14 billion (£4.6 bn.) or, more than 20 per cent of East Germany's total annual investments . . . Western specialists acknowledged the feat but said that unlike Siemens in West Germany which was able quickly to achieve volume production of its own chips and could use them in its own products, East Germany might have been better off buying the chips far more cheaply on the world market.[113]

The transition from state to multinational capitalism would thus require dismantling many of the organizational structures built up to promote economic development in isolation from the world market. But many Eastern managers would emerge from this process as beneficiaries, particularly if, as in the case of the bosses of the *Kombinate*, they could expect to attach themselves to one of the great power-houses of the world economy. There would also be many losers among the less competent and nimble managers and perhaps especially in the central economic apparatus of the old bureaucratic command system. But the entire history of capitalism is that of restructurings in which the less efficient members of the ruling class itself are eliminated. The 1970s and 1980s had been a time of enormous upheaval in the West, involving a considerable reorganization of corporate structures in response to global recessions, intensified international competition, and the boom in financial speculation. The changes in the East were in many respects a concentrated version of the same process, as the last and greatest stronghold of the autarkic economic development that had been the global norm between the 1930s and the 1950s was finally cracked open.

The social meaning of the East European revolutions was obscured by their most visible aspect, the collapse of the Stalinist one-party states. But an economically dominant class must be distinguished from the specific political form through which it both secures its own cohesion and establishes its rule over society. The German bourgeoisie remained economically dominant throughout the twentieth century, despite a succession of changes of political regime – the quasi-absolutist Second Reich, the parliamentary Weimar Republic, the Nazi dictatorship, and finally the Bundesrepublik. The relationship between ruling class and political regime had been especially intimate under Stalinism – the very name often given that class referred to the *nomenklatura* system through which the party leadership made appointments to key positions. Nevertheless, the one-party state provided the political framework through which the dominant class of bureaucrats, managers, generals, and secret policemen exercised their social power. The difference between the party and the ruling class was dramatically demonstrated during the heyday of Solidarność in 1980–1. Under the pressure of working-class revolt, the structures of party rule cracked and the party itself disintegrated. The state, however, did not – in particular, the repressive apparatuses of the army and security services held together and provided the command structures and coercive resources needed to mount the military coup of December 1981. One noteworthy feature of the revolutions of 1989 was how little they affected the repressive state apparatus. Indeed the military in certain cases helped promote change. In Poland General Jaruzelski, the architect of the 1981 coup, and the Interior Minister and chief administrator of martial law,

General Kiszczak, played a crucial role in negotiating the round-table agreement with Solidarność and the formation of the Mazowiecki coalition government (under which they continued to hold office). In Romania, the army chiefs' decision to side with the popular rising against a regime whose dynastic, personal character had isolated it even from the bulk of the *nomenklatura* guaranteed the success of the Christmas Revolution. Even the secret police showed no sign of simply disappearing. The East German Stasi came under the most pressure (though the opposition New Forum sought to defend its offices against popular anger), but elsewhere the old security apparatuses – the StB in Czechoslovakia, even the Romanian Securitate – appeared to be carrying on under new management. Contrary to what Anderson requires of a revolution, the 'old state apparatus' was not 'decisively ended' by the collapse of Stalinism.

The substantial continuity both in the core apparatuses of state power and in the personnel of the ruling class itself indicates the limits of the political upheavals in Eastern Europe. They represented a change in political regime rather than in social system. Trotsky had drawn an important distinction between 'social revolutions' such as those 'which substituted the bourgeois for the feudal regime' and 'political revolutions which, without destroying the economic foundations of society, swept out an old ruling upper crust (1830 and 1848 in France, February 1917 in Russia, etc.)'.[114] He believed that the popular overthrow of Stalinism would amount to such a political revolution, since it would leave intact the 'economic foundations' of the workers' state established in October 1917 and not destroyed despite its subsequent bureaucratic degeneration. The Stalinist regimes in Eastern Europe were indeed brought down by political revolutions, but not of the kind anticipated by Trotsky. The capitalist mode of production, whose bureaucratic state-capitalist form had been established in the USSR during the Stalin counter-revolution of 1928–32 and extended to Eastern Europe after 1945, remained dominant after the revolutions. Their achievement was to effect a political reorganization of the ruling class which would allow the East European economies' full integration into the world market and the restructuring required by the transition from state to multinational capitalism.

Of course, the millions who took to the streets throughout Eastern Europe in the autumn and winter of 1989 did not do so because they sought such a move sideways, from one variant of capitalism to another. They had taken the considerable risks involved, especially in the early phase of the popular movements, because their rulers were visibly weakened by the changes under way in the USSR. Inspired by example and by their own successes, they developed a growing sense of autonomy, of the ability to remake their own lives. Their triumph was a great act of self-liberation which, both in itself and because of the greater political liberties it brought in its wake, could only be welcomed and celebrated. Inevitably, however, the popular movements in Eastern Europe had been profoundly influenced by what had become the consensus among both pro-regime and opposition intellectuals as a result of the progressive decay of 'Marxist-Leninist' ideology, that the market economies prevailing in the West provided the only framework for political liberty and material progress.

These hopes were likely to be dashed. Two reports in April 1990 underlined the difficulties involved in restructuring the East European economies. The Institute for International Finance pointed out that Eastern Europe, with 2.5 per cent of the world's population, 2 per cent of world output, exports amounting to three-quarters of Hong Kong's, and a hard-currency debt amounting already to one quarter of Latin America's, was hardly a particularly attractive site for Western investment. Fresh private loans were likely to be limited in extent, while direct investment by Western multinationals would be highly selective and concentrated in the most advanced economies – East Germany, Hungary and Czechoslovakia.[115] The United Nations Commission for Europe cast doubt on the ability of the East European economies to absorb the kind of state aid promised by the European Community. It also expressed concern about the social consequences of restructuring, warning, according to the *Financial Times*, that '[t]he social consensus in favour of reform could be threatened if the initial gains from tough restructuring measures went to service foreign debt rather than to domestic investment and personal consumption'. Privatization 'might simply transform a public monopoly into a private one' and lead to 'large transfers of wealth either to old managers and former *nomenklatura* members or to Western newcomers'.[116]

The immediate future in Eastern Europe is less likely to be some idealized version of the most prosperous of the Western liberal democracies – West Germany or Switzerland – than a condition approximating that of the more developed Latin American economies. Countries such as Brazil and Argentina benefited in the mid-1980s from the replacement of military dictatorships by liberal parliamentary regimes. This political liberalization took place, however, against the background of the debt crisis, which led to the imposition of austerity measures slashing output, income, and employment. The new parliamentary regimes were thus weak ones, presiding over the profound social crisis created by large-scale pauperization and confronted with political challenges, from both the right (the Argentine military) and the left (Brazil's powerful and militant workers' movement). The new regimes in Eastern Europe in all probability will take the form also of weak liberal democracies threatened by large-scale social and political instability – a future resembling the region's past in the inter-war years, when the new states produced by the collapse of the Central European empires for the most part oscillated between feeble parliamentary regimes and military dictatorships.

The post-Stalinist governments enjoyed, however, one signal advantage, namely that they were drawn largely from the old opposition movements. Tim Garton Ash shrewdly observed of Poland:

> The prime minister, the labour minister, the Citizens' Parliamentary Club, the chief editor of *Gazeta Wyborcza*, not to mention Lech Wałeşa, were quite unquestionably men of Solidarity. If they now appealed to the workers – 'Don't strike! Accept factory closures! Take a real cut in wages!' – they had a better chance of being listened to than anyone else, just because the workers knew that these men, above all others, had fought for their rights over the last ten years.[117]

The resulting situation was full of ironies, as ex-Marxists like the Labour Minister, Jacek Kuroń, and *Gazeta Wyborcza* editor Adam Michnik opposed anti-austerity strikes which were supported by the OPZZ, the old Stalinist state unions. Although the Mazowiecki government's huge political capital allowed it to retain popular support for restructuring measures which its Stalinist predecessor under Mieczysław Rakowski had been unable to implement, the great enthusiasms of 1980–1 were far in the past. Solidarność, legalized again, only attracted two million members, a fraction of the ten million of its heyday. Integrating the East European economies in the world market would clearly involve major reductions in employment and living standards – East Germany's incorporation into the Federal Republic was expected to cause a rise in unemployment to two million, 20–25 per cent of the workforce in the East.[118] Even a government as popular as the sainted Václav Havel's hesitated before such measures – the two leading economic ministers in the Czechoslovak government, Komarek and Klaus, were deeply divided over how rapidly to implement austerity policies. Politics in the East European successor regimes began in the spring of 1990 to fragment, despite the widely shared assumption that a transition to a market economy represented the only way forward: the fanatical followers of Hayek and Friedman found themselves confronted with a variety of forces which sought to moderate the impact of Thatcherite 'shock therapy' – social-democrats such as Havel and Michnik, and authoritarian nationalists such as Wałesa and the Hungarian Democratic Forum – as well as with reconstructed Stalinist parties which were in some cases (for example, Czechoslovakia and East Germany) to retain a popular base by exploiting justifiable fears aroused by the new government's austerity measures. The resulting conflicts, which began in Poland to tear Solidarność apart, would in all likelihood become more polarized in the years ahead. The clashes in Bucharest in June 1990 between miners loyal to the ruling National Salvation Front, which had almost trebled their wages, and radical democrats opposed to the consolidation of *nomenklatura* power in a new guise were a portent. Eastern Europe faced after its liberation, not the prospect of contented and prosperous capitalist democracy, but a future of economic crisis, social conflict and political instability.

The same contradiction between economic and political liberalization made itself felt within the USSR. The conditions for a political transition to liberal democracy were much less favourable there than in Eastern Europe. The Soviet economy, far larger and more self-sufficient than those of Eastern Europe, is also far more insulated from the world market. The USSR's exports in 1988 amounted to $110.51 billion, compared to a total gross national product of $2,154.8 billion. Moreover, convertible currency exports amounted to a mere $39 billion, much less than Taiwan's or Sweden's, and only 47 per cent of which were manufactured goods.[119] The country's vast industries were closely integrated into the structures of the bureaucratic command economy. Unravelling these structures to achieve the rises in productivity which participation in the international division of labour makes possible would involve enormous disruption and undermine the power of a *nomenklatura* with sixty years' experience of managing a huge closed economy. The conservative resistance within the bureaucracy was therefore far more substantial than in Eastern Europe – and there was, of course, no external power whose withdrawal of support could break the back of such resistance, the fate of Honecker and Jakeš at Gorbachev's hands.

At the same time, the enormous popular radicalization which swept the USSR at the end of the 1980s endangered the position of conservatives and reformers alike. The secessionist movements in

Transcaucasia and the Baltic republics threatened to break up the USSR. The radical democrats of the Popular Fronts in the Russian Federation itself were undermining the control of local party bosses. And, most ominous of all, there was the economic crisis. The attempts to graft market mechanisms on to the bureaucratic command economy offered the worst of both worlds: the old structures broke down without new ones to emerge to replace them. In 1989 GNP actually fell. The miners' strikes of July and August that year conjured up the threat of a Soviet Solidarność. One mining manager said during the Siberian strikes: 'People do not have what they were guaranteed. People have nothing worthwhile, no housing, no food, no leisure facilities.'[120] Economic grievances could easily acquire a political focus. Miners striking in Vorkuta in November 1989 demanded not only improvements in wages and conditions but the repeal of article 6 of the Soviet Constitution, which guaranteed the Communist Party's political monopoly. The East European revolutions themselves must also have concentrated the minds of the entire bureaucracy, as it contemplated the fate of Erich Honecker and Nicolae Ceauşescu.

It is hardly surprising that in these circumstances the conservative wing of the *nomenklatura* should become increasingly assertive. The February 1990 Central Committee plenum saw fierce attacks on Gorbachev, notably by the ambassador to Poland, Vladimir Brovikov, who asked: 'It is said that the people back *perestroika*, but which *perestroika*? The one that for the past five years has brought us into crisis, anarchy and economic decay?'[121] The Leningrad party chief, Boris Gidaspov, called for the formation of a separate Russian Communist Party to counter the rise of the nationalist movements in Transcaucasia and the Prebaltic.[122] The conservatives also lent their backing to the right-wing Russian nationalist groups – the various squabbling splinters of the neo-fascist Pamyat movement, but, more importantly, a network of 'military-patriotic' clubs for youth led by veterans of the Afghan war and promoted by the Komsomol Central Committee, and the United Front of the Working People of Russia (OFT), which sought to exploit the discontent created by Gorbachev's economic policies.[123] Nevertheless, the conservatives did not break with Gorbachev and indeed voted at the February 1990 plenum to scrap article 6 and end the party's monopoly: the only vote against this decision came from the radical democrat Boris Yeltsin, because it did not go far enough. The vote was greeted with euphoria in the West: the London *Independent* carried the headline: 'End of the Communist state'.[124] This reaction obscured the real considerations involved in the decision to abolish article 6 – a grudging acceptance of the fact that a multiparty system was developing anyway, made more palatable to the conservatives because of the increasingly authoritarian course taken by Gorbachev himself.

Twenty years earlier Chris Harman had noted how the struggle between reformers and conservatives within the Stalinist regimes in Eastern Europe

> permits, even encourages, extra-bureaucratic classes (above all the workers) to mobilize, at first behind the slogans of the 'reforming bureaucracy', but increasingly on their own account ... The 'reformers' having come to power try to ride the storm. But they can do so only by reasserting the basic class structure of the society. This means destroying whatever gains the workers have made. At first the 'cold' method of ideological hegemony is used (e.g. Gomutka successfully, and Nagy, unsuccessfully, in 1956 and Dubček in 1968); if this fails, then the 'hot' method of armed repression, based upon Russian troops follows (Kádár in 1956, Husak in 1969).[125]

Although the challenges to the Soviet reformers of the late 1980s and early 1990s came on various fronts, and not simply from workers, the dynamic analysed by Harman can be seen at work in Gorbachev's steady movement towards the use of 'hot methods' to restore stability. Among the early signs of this reorientation was his decision to ditch Yeltsin, then the most outspoken reformer in the party leadership, in October 1987. In 1989 Gorbachev tolerated the overthrow of Stalinism in Eastern Europe, but sanctioned increased repression in the USSR itself – the brutal attack by troops on a nationalist demonstration in Tiblisi in April, for example, and the introduction of legislation severely punishing the organizers of 'unauthorized demonstrations' and limiting the right to strike. These measures did not allow the centre to reimpose its control, but other steps were taken in preparation for the use of more rigorous forms of coercion – for example, the transfer of crack army units withdrawn from Afghanistan to the internal security forces of the KGB and the Ministry of the Interior.

The turning point in this shift towards 'hot methods' arguably came in January 1990, when Moscow sent a large military force to take control of Baku, the capital of Azerbaijan. The pretext for armed intervention was provided by fighting between Armenians and Azeris over the disputed region of Nagorno-Karabakh: the military occupation of Baku was necessary, on this account, to prevent pogroms taking place – a theme calculated to go down well in Washington and other Western capitals obsessed with Islamic fundamentalism, since the Azeris were Muslims and the Armenians Christians. The real aim of the operation was to crush the independence movement in Azerbaijan, led by the Popular Front, whose growing militancy was demonstrated by the Azeri reaction to the breaching of the Berlin Wall, which was to tear down the border fences separating the republic from Iran. The Defence Minister of the USSR, General Dimitri Yazov, let the cat out of the bag when he told *Izvestia* that the Popular Front had taken power in Azerbaijan and that 'our task is . . . to destroy this structure of power'.[126] This clear indication of Moscow's willingness to use force to hold the USSR together was followed by mounting pressures directed against the independence movements in the Baltic republics.

Gorbachev's election in March 1990 to the new post of executive President, armed with extensive emergency powers, was part of the same process. The Congress of People's Deputies and its standing body, the Supreme Soviet, enjoyed considerably greater legitimacy, thanks to their origin in relatively free elections, than the old party structures. By increasingly associating himself with a partially liberalized state Gorbachev could acquire greater authority for his policies. Moreover, by detaching himself from the party, and developing new state decision-making bodies such as the Presidential Council, Gorbachev could by-pass some of the obstacles to economic reform mounted by conservatives within the bureaucracy. In November 1989, Leonid Abalkin, the Deputy Prime Minister responsible for economic reform, unveiled proposals for the 'consistent denationalization of property', gradual adjustment of prices to world-market levels, the establishment of financial and currency markets, and the encouragement of foreign investment.[127] But the implementation of these measures was blocked by the Prime Minister, Nikolai Ryzhkov, who instead introduced in early December an emergency package strengthening the centre's control over enterprises' investment, pricing, and foreign trade and put off increases in official prices till 1992.

This reluctance to push through the kind of economic restructuring already under way in Eastern Europe did not simply reflect the vested interests of bureaucrats in the industrial ministries and planning apparatus. Reformers and conservatives alike were terrified of the reaction from a population already embittered by the economic privations accompanying the rhetoric of *perestroika* to large-scale layoffs and price increases. One response was what Boris Kagarlitsky called 'market Stalinism.' He cited as an example the economists Igor

Klyamkin and Andranik Migranyan, who argued that 'the sole means of implementing a liberal economic reform is the creation of a strong, authoritarian regime capable of effectively suppressing the resistance of the masses'.[128] Gorbachev's accession to the executive Presidency marked a shift on his part towards such a strategy. His personal economic adviser, Nikolai Petrakov, appointed in February 1990, advocated the creation of a 'normal market economy', involving the destruction of the 'Soviet super-monopolists' of the industrial ministries, a 'drastic reduction in state investment programmes', price rises and a wage freeze.[129] One parliamentary economist predicted in April 1990 that the government would implement reforms doubling prices by the beginning of the next year and wiping out ten million jobs.[130] It was perhaps an indication of the authoritarianism required to force through such measures that Gorbachev should include in his new Presidential Council representatives of the extreme right such as the (aptly named) writer Valentin Rasputin.

Gorbachev thus increasingly assumed the kind of role analysed by the classical Marxist theory of Bonapartism – a figure concentrating enormous executive power in his hands as he sought to balance between the main social and political forces, reformers and conservatives, masses and bureaucracy. The radical-democratic opposition represented by the Inter-regional Group of Deputies was hampered from effectively challenging the direction in which he now seemed to be taking the USSR by their own acceptance of liberal ideology. Thus Yeltsin, elevated to the Presidency of the Russian Federation in May 1990, effectively renounced even paying lip-service to Marxist-Leninist ideology, declaring: 'I support private ownership of production means and land' and calling for a 'new model' embracing 'the achievements of Western democracy'.[131] But there were cross-currents as well. Gorbachev called the miners' strikes of July and August 1989 'perhaps the worst ordeal to befall our country in all four years of restructuring'.[132] The hardships and disillusionment of *perestroika* had promoted the development of independent working-class organizations for the first time since the decline of the original soviets after 1917. A number of trade-union organizations sprang up outside the official apparatus. One of the most important was Sotsprof, the Federation of Independent Socialist Trade Unions. This grouping was effectively an alliance between left-wing intellectuals organized in the Committee for a New Socialist Party and the miners' strike committees in the Donbass, Kuzbass and Vorkuta coalfields. One Sotsprof activist, Oleg Voronin, described the federation's basic demands as 'workers' self-management, collective ownership of the

means of production, democratic planning from below' – a programme setting it in frontal opposition to both conservative and reforming
wings of the *nomenklatura.*[133] The Socialist Party of the USSR
embodying these ideas was established in June 1990. Sixty years after
the destruction of the Left Opposition, authentic working-class
politics was reviving in the land of the October Revolution.

3
THE TRIUMPH OF THE WEST?

'Whoever speaks of Europe is mistaken.'

Prince Otto von Bismarck

3.1 BACK TO THE FUTURE?

Many who did not share Francis Fukuyama's rather esoteric philosophical assumptions nevertheless accepted the conclusion that he
drew from the crisis of Stalinism, namely that it amounted to 'the
ultimate triumph of Western liberal democracy', the 'unabashed
victory of economic and political liberalism'.[1] One can distinguish
three distinct components involved in this claim. First, there is the
thought, which I discuss in the following chapter, that there is no
longer any plausible alternative to liberal-democratic capitalism as a
social model. Secondly, there is the idea that the disintegration of the
Eastern bloc and the erosion of Soviet power correlatively strengthen
Western capitalism in general and the United States in particular – a
view summed up by media claims that the US has won the Cold War.
Finally, there is the belief that continued economic expansion in the
West combined with the opening up of the East marks the beginning
of a new boom era for world capitalism. I happen to think that all
three claims are false: in this chapter I subject the latter two to critical
examination.

Any assessment of the impact of the collapse of Stalinism on the
world system must start with some appraisal of the state of the global
economy and more especially of the Western capitalist countries still
forming its core. After the most sustained and powerful period of
growth in the history of capitalism, the long boom of the 1950s and
1960s (world gross national product rose three and a half times
between 1948 and 1973), the world system entered in the late 1960s
into the worst period of instability it had suffered since the Great
Depression of the inter-war era. Two major and generalized recessions afflicted the world economy in 1974–5 and 1979–82. To the

classical symptoms of slump – falling or stagnating output, rising unemployment – was added a new and alarming phenomenon: recessions were marked by an acceleration in the rate of inflation, threatening the collapse of the financial system and exacerbating social conflict. In the mid-1970s especially, when the end of the long boom coincided with an escalation of class struggle throughout Western Europe whose high point was the Portuguese Revolution of 1974–5, it seemed as if the twentieth century had become once again 'the epoch of wars and revolutions' that the Communist International had described in the aftermath of October 1917.[2]

In the event, the pattern of the 1970s was not repeated in the following decade. A sharp recovery from recession in the United States in 1983–4 was transmitted to the rest of the advanced economies, opening what seemed to be a new phase of growth. Despite upsets – above all, the great scare of Black Monday, 19 October 1987, the day of the second Wall Street crash – the recovery continued unbroken throughout the decade. By the autumn of 1989 the *Financial Times* could report that '[n]ormally cautious officials in the world's finance ministries and central banks can now be heard to whisper the previously unthinkable: that the world might be on the edge of a new golden age'.[3] Such expectations, reinforced by the impact of the East European revolutions, translated themselves into euphoria on the world's leading stock markets, which greeted the 1990s with a major surge in share prices.

Even before the upheavals in the East, many on the left had come to believe that capitalism had successfully reorganized itself so as to overcome the problems responsible for the crises of the 1970s and early 1980s and to lay the basis for another long boom comparable to those of the mid-nineteenth and twentieth centuries. Various expressions were coined to describe this new phase of capitalist development – for example, 'postFordism' and 'flexible accumulation'.[4] These theories were, however, mistaken. For one thing, they failed adequately to explore the causes first of slump and then of recovery in the 1970s and 1980s. It was a deep-seated crisis of profitability which precipitated the two great recessions of the past twenty years. The *Financial Times* acknowledged that 'the postwar boom began to peter out in the late 1960s, not, as is commonly thought, as a result of the 1973–4 oil shock. The clearest guide to the underlying trend is ... profit ratios, in which a serious decline is visible already in the late 1960s, for many of the major economies'.[5] Such a fall in the rate of profit is precisely what Marx believed to be the main cause of economic crises.

But it is far from obvious that the global economic recovery which set in after 1982 reflected the kind of comprehensive restructuring – in particular, the wholesale destruction of less efficient capital – which would be required for an increase in the rate of profit sustainable in the long term. The limited character of the recovery in profitability which did take place is indicated by the enormous surge in various forms of financial investment: taking over firms and selling off their assets and speculation in securities and real estate proved to be more attractive than investment in more efficient plant and equipment, while the atmosphere of a bull market helped promote new forms of speculative investment reflected in the vogue for leveraged buy-outs and junk bonds. For all the globalization of capital, the most important engine of growth proved to be Keynesian demand management by a state which remained remarkably interventionist despite the supposed intellectual hegemony of the neo-liberal economics of Friedman and Hayek. The US economic recovery was in the first place the unexpected result of what has been dubbed the 'military Keynesianism' of the Reagan administration – tax cuts and higher defence spending helped stimulate demand just at the moment when the Federal Reserve Board relaxed its monetary policy to avert bank collapses after Mexico had defaulted on its debt in August 1982. Most major Western governments introduced packages of measures designed further to boost demand when a marked economic slowdown in 1986 seemed to augur a third major recession. And the main central banks cut interest rates and eased monetary policy in response to Black Monday. The renewed emphasis on a politically managed world economy was underlined by the efforts of the Group of Seven (G7 – the US, Japan, West Germany, France, Britain, Italy, and Canada) to co-ordinate policies, especially after the February 1987 Louvre Accord committed them to stabilizing the major currencies.

The undoubted achievements of this interventionism, notably in containing the impact of the 1987 stock market crash, did not alter the fact that it served primarily to manage a set of conflicts which the recovery had not solved, and indeed had if anything exacerbated. Of these, the most important was the relative economic decline of the United States. Overwhelmingly the dominant economy at the end of the Second World War, the US subsequently saw its position progressively eroded – a process matched by the rise (or revival) of other major industrial economies, notably Japan and West Germany. In 1965 US share of world GNP was still 39.3 per cent: by 1987 it had fallen to 30.1 per cent. During the same period Japan's share rose from 5.2 to 15.9 per cent and West Germany's from 6.6 to 7.4 per cent.[6] The resulting shift in global economic power underlay the currency instabilities of the 1960s which prepared the way for the roller-coaster the world economy rode in the 1970s and early 1980s. The period of economic recovery thereafter underlined the imbalances between the US and its major Western rivals: higher defence spending in the early Reagan years was financed by increased borrowing; the hike in interest rates to attract foreign borrowers helped to keep the dollar high on the foreign exchanges, further undermining the competitiveness of US manufacturing industry. The result was the 'twin deficits' which became chronic features of the American economy in the 1980s – huge deficits in both the federal budget and the current balance of payments which reduced the US to the status of a debtor nation for the first time since the First World War.

The most serious potential conflict created by this state of affairs was that between the US and Japan. The relationship between the two powers appeared to be tipping in the latter's favour. For one thing, the US balance of trade deficit with Japan remained chronically high even when the decline of the dollar in 1985–7 stimulated a general rise in American exports. The 1988 deficit of $35 billion reflected Japanese firms' ability to penetrate a wide range of domestic American markets – vehicles, machine tools, consumer electronics, semiconductors.[7] Secondly, Japanese direct investment in the US (totalling $71.9 billion in March 1988), in part an attempt to defuse American protectionist pressures by replacing Japanese exports with locally assembled products, instead fed nationalist fears of the loss of US economic independence.[8] Finally, the huge outflow of Japanese capital in the 1980s helped finance the US deficits. The Chicago economist David Hale saw this as part of a broader strategy on Tokyo's part:

> Since the mid-1980s, the overwhelming priority of Japanese public policy has been to promote international economic harmony by helping the US to cope with the financial tensions created by America's large government deficits, low private savings, and permissive financial deregulation. First, the Japanese pursued highly stimulative macroeconomic policies after 1986 and more than doubled the level of manufacturing imports. Second, during the dollar crises of the late 1980s, Japan intervened on a large scale to help stabilize US financial markets. The Japanese ministry of finance purchased nearly $60 billion of US dollar securities. The Japanese central bank attempted to restrict credit growth not through rising interest rates but through administrative controls on bank lending. The finance ministry requested the big Tokyo insurance companies to stop selling US treasury bonds.[9]

But the scale of Japanese financial and economic power, even when it was used to remedy the defects of American policy, exacerbated the near-paranoia displayed by wide sectors of US opinion. By 1989 American opinion polls were showing that half the electorate regarded Japanese economic power as a greater threat to the US than Soviet military strength. These popular attitudes were echoed in (often only marginally) more sophisticated forms by policy-makers in Washington. Political support was thus provided for a variety of mercantilist measures – federal promotion of strategically important industries (for example, the Congress-sponsored Sematech consortium to improve semiconductor technology), the invocation against Japan of the 'Super 101' provision authorizing retaliation for 'unfair trade practices' under the Omnibus Trade Act 1988, and the bilateral negotiations between Washington and Tokyo under the Structural Impediments Initiative. These and other protectionist tensions involving the major trading economies – for example, the disputes between the US and the European Community (EC) over the latter's Common Agricultural Policy – led the *Financial Times* to lament in September 1989:

> the world's trading system is noticeably less free than it was ten years ago ... The growing concern in the US and Europe that they are losing the race with the Japanese and the newly industrializing countries, predominantly in south-east Asia, has spawned ... a revival in protectionism unrivalled since the 1930s.[10]

Serious and growing though these tensions among the advanced economies were, all benefited, albeit to unequal degrees, from the recovery after 1982. The same could not be said of the rest of the world. The debt crisis precipitated by Mexico's default in August 1982 caused appalling suffering in most of the Third World. New loans to debtor states dried up, while debt rescheduling agreements between these states and their Western creditors led to a continuing flow of repayments from South to North. The result – a net transfer of value from poor to rich countries – went largely unnoticed, despite the moral outrage it constituted. Thus in 1985 new long-term lending to the developing countries of $35 billion was exceeded by an outflow of almost $58 billion in interest payments on existing loans to Western banks.[11] By 1986 debt servicing payments exceeded new loans to Latin America since 1982 by almost $100 billion, wiping out the entire net inflow of capital to this region during the 1970s.[12] Per capita income in the most indebted countries fell by 1.8 per cent a year during the first half of the 1980s.[13] Only the East Asian NICs –

chiefly the 'Four Tigers' (South Korea, Taiwan, Hong Kong, and
Singapore), but also such emerging exporters of manufactured goods
as Malaysia, Indonesia, and Thailand – broke out of this pattern. The
prodigious growth of the Pacific Rim economies in the 1980s
provided the basis of projections according to which by the end of the
century the East Asian states would have a joint GNP greater than
Western Europe's and as great as North America's.[14] But if a handful
of economies were climbing out of the Third World, whole continents
– above all subsaharan Africa – seemed to be slipping backwards. The
World Bank reported at the end of 1989: 'Overall Africans are as
poor today as they were thirty years ago.'[15]

The recovery of the 1980s thus widened the gap between the core
and the periphery of the world economy. There were, in any case,
grave doubts about how long that recovery could continue. It had
been marked by a pronounced dislocation between the often uneven
and sluggish growth of manufacturing industry and the spectacular
rise of world stock markets, above all in the main centres of Wall
Street, Tokyo, and the City of London. The speculative impetus of
financial markets seemed able to brush off setbacks such as Black
Monday and another brief but terrifying crash on Wall Street almost
exactly two years later, on 13 October 1989. But by February 1990
Anthony Harris was describing from Washington 'the financial
apocalypse which is being revealed by increasingly frequent instal-
ments' as the great credit boom unravelled in the US – for example,
the bankruptcy of much of the savings and loan industry, itself
intricately bound up with the long overdue collapse of the junk bonds
market, and in turn threatening the investment portfolios of insurance
companies and pension schemes, an addition to the federal government's liabilities of between $300 and $800 billion. 'At first sight',
Harris observed, 'the US economy may appear to be shrugging off
these disasters with comical unconcern, like one of those characters in
a cartoon film who keep walking for several strides after they have
stepped off the precipice.' But the apparent stability was misleading,
since '[a]ll other markets are being sustained at the moment by the
huge outflow [of capital] from Tokyo'. Should the Japanese stock
exchange falter, 'the financial markets could soon face the shock
which normally follows a cartoon double-take'.[16] Within weeks of
these words being written, the great Japanese financial boom had
come to an end, as thirty per cent was wiped off the value of stocks
and bonds on the Tokyo market. Perhaps state intervention would
once again avert another recession by preventing the gyrations of the
money markets from dragging down the real economy, but it seemed

hard to believe that the great house of cards erected in the 1980s could survive indefinitely.

What impact would the full integration of the East European economies into the world economy have on this state of affairs? Once the initial euphoria after the opening of the Berlin Wall had dissipated, hard calculations suggested that the effect would be at best neutral, at worst negative. At the beginning of March 1990 the *Financial Times* reported that 'Western commercial banks, while applauding economic and political reform in eastern Europe, are privately expressing reluctance to extend new loans to the region for any purpose except specific project finance'. This attitude, reflecting a pessimistic assessment of the prospects of the East European economies, was matched by an equally bleak appraisal of the effect of integrating them into the world market by a British investment banker quoted in the same issue of the *Financial Times*. Jonathan Wilmot of Crédit Suisse First Boston predicted that 'a mild recession in the US, 10,000 points off Tokyo's Nikkei stock exchange index, a doubling of the West German budget deficit and strains within the European Monetary System may be the price the West has to pay for reconstructing eastern Europe.' All might be consequences of the inflationary impact on a world economy close to full capacity of the investments and subsidies required to ease the transition in Eastern Europe.[17] If Western bankers were unprepared to make the necessary loans, multinationals seemed likely to engage in what one consultant called 'cherrypicking' – highly selective investment in the most efficient sectors – even in the most favourable case of West German companies moving into East Germany.[18] Even if some of these prognoses proved to be too pessimistic, the overall picture they suggested conformed closely to the general pattern of Western investment in the postwar era, in which the advanced economies primarily invested in each other – a pattern reinforced by the effective withdrawal of foreign capital from much of the Third World as a result of the debt crisis.[19]

Beyond any specific economic consequences, the overall effect of reintegrating Eastern Europe into the world market would, in all probability, destabilize the international state-system. Underpinning that system since the Second World War had been the division of the world between two politico-military blocs headed by the great continental powers, the US and the USSR. The global balance of forces had at all times favoured the Western alliance, embracing as it did by far the wealthier of the two superpowers, as well as the advanced economies of Western Europe and Japan; willy-nilly much of the rest of the world had fallen within its orbit. The relative economic decline of the US and the stagnation of the USSR placed this bipolar arrangement under increasing pressure. By the late 1980s Paul Kennedy could write: 'it is plain that there already exists a *multi*polar world once more, if one measures the economic indices alone.' Kennedy discerned 'five large politico-economic "power-centres" – China, Japan, the EEC, the Soviet Union and the United States itself'.[20]

In fact, the situation was considerably more complex than might appear from the economic evidence of superpower decline. Japan and West Germany had indeed significantly eroded the economic supremacy enjoyed by the US at the end of the Second World War. At the same time, however, American politico-military leadership of the Western capitalist bloc continued largely unchallenged into the 1980s. US hegemony was in two crucial respects a condition of West European and Japanese economic success. First, the politico-military integration of the advanced countries under the leadership of Washington created a very large economic space (accounting in 1987 for some two-thirds of world trade in manufactured goods) in which competition between capitals could be pursued with a large degree of freedom and without the risk of developing into the kind of armed conflict which twice devastated the globe in the first half of the century.[21] Secondly, the military preponderance of the US played a crucial role in its relative economic decline: high levels of defence spending diverted investment from civilian industry and thus contributed to low rates of growth of productivity and output throughout the postwar era. At the same time, the comparatively low proportions of GNP devoted to military expenditure in Japan and West Germany helped make possible the very high levels of investment which enormously enhanced the competitiveness of these countries' industries.[22]

There was thus a kind of symbiosis between American politico-military hegemony and the economic rise of Japan and Western Europe. This led to a growing level of tension between the US and its allies – over trade, nuclear strategy, relations with the Eastern bloc – but at the same time tended to stabilize the situation. The division of labour within the Western bloc helped keep European and Japanese military commitments comparatively low. Moreover, Washington's response to the signs of its decline – most dramatically evident in the US defeat in Vietnam and the wave of Third World revolutions during the 1970s culminating in the victory of the Sandinistas in Nicaragua – was significantly to increase defence spending and more generally to assert its global political role, a process begun under the Carter administration but continued with gusto by Ronald Reagan.[23] The expansion of defence expenditure in the late 1970s and early 1980s if anything accelerated the relative economic decline of the US but it nevertheless served to reinforce the existing pattern of relationships within the Western bloc. If the world was evidently by the 1980s economically multipolar, politically it was still bipolar. But the East European revolutions looked set to change all that.

It was the sudden, wholly unexpected return of the German Question to the top of the agenda of international politics which most immediately threatened to crack open the postwar division of the world. After all, it had been the growing imbalance between German economic and military power and that of its main rivals, Britain and France, which had first destabilized the European state-system at the turn of the nineteenth century, and then caused it twice to implode, dragging in what Kennedy calls the 'offstage superpowers', those two vast, Europeanized continental states, the US and Russia.[24] A necessary condition of the superpowers' domination after 1945 was the partition between them of Europe, which ensured that the single most economically advanced region in the world occupied a politically subordinate status. The linchpin of this arrangement was the division and military occupation of Germany, which helped to keep in a secondary role the one European country capable of playing the part of a Great Power on the global stage.

The collapse of the German Democratic Republic and its consequent incorporation into the Federal Republic threatened to bring in its wake dramatic changes in the international state-system. This was not primarily because of any major enhancement of German economic power which reunification would entail. West Germany was already in the late 1980s the world's largest exporter. It was also the economic hub of the European Community, far and away the biggest trading bloc in the world (in 1987 the EC accounted for 43.1 per cent of world trade in manufactured goods, Japan 13.0 per cent, the US 10.5 per cent).[25] When a rise in West German interest rates was followed throughout the rest of Western Europe in October 1989, the *Financial Times* commented: 'Europe already has a central bank. It is called the Bundesbank and it is located in Frankfurt.'[26] In itself, the reunification of Germany would not dramatically alter this state of affairs. On one estimate, the manufacturing sector of a united Germany would be 85 per cent of the size of those of France, Italy, and Britain combined, while that of West Germany was already 68 per cent.[27]

The impact of German reunification was far more likely to be political, in increasing the confidence and assertiveness of a ruling class which could now claim an international role commensurate with its economic power. This sea-change was bluntly expressed by Alfred Herrhausen, chief executive of Deutsche Bank, days before his assassination by the Red Army Faction in November 1989: 'Germany, a reunified Germany, will be an enormous, strong economic force ... and when you as a bank are strongly positioned within this country, then I think you are destined to play a major role in global banking.'[28] Herrhausen's close associate Helmut Kohl, the West German Chancellor, rapidly began to flex his muscles. His ten-point plan for reunification, unveiled in November 1989 within weeks of the opening of the Berlin Wall, made scant reference to the Western alliance and was drawn up without consulting Kohl's NATO partners, leading a British official to wonder 'whether the German card had not already been played'.[29] One sign that it had was Kohl's insistence the following March on linking a German guarantee of the Oder–Neisse line marking East Germany's postwar border with Poland to Warsaw's renunciation of its claims for war reparations. Kohl retreated before the ensuing uproar, but not before his stance had provoked the formation of a Franco-Polish alignment recalling the Petite Entente of the inter-war years. The prospect of a reunited Germany led the Mazowiecki government to reappraise the role in Eastern Europe of what till recently it had regarded as Poland's Russian oppressor. Thus, Polish negotiators at the Vienna talks on conventional force reductions opposed a NATO proposal that Soviet 'storage units' (back-up units kept well below strength in peacetime) in the western USSR should be kept at five per cent of wartime manpower. An East European diplomat explained: 'It is the fear of the Bundeswehr as well as NATO's considerable storage units, which has made the Poles very anxious about their own future security interests.'[30] The row over the Oder–Neisse line provoked the Polish government to call for Russian troops to remain in East Germany.

The axis between Moscow, Warsaw – and Paris – against Bonn over Germany's eastern borders showed how silly Tim Garton Ash was to claim that 'there was only one bloc – the Soviet one', 'a bloc of dictatorships under the central command of an imperial dictatorship', while 'NATO was, and is, a voluntary alliance of democracies.'[31] Great-Power interests had forged the two alliances and would survive the collapse of Stalinism. Indeed, the new situation threatened *both* alliances. This wasn't simply because of the realignments precipitated by the prospect of German reunification. The fall of the Stalinist regimes in Eastern Europe and the Russian military withdrawal which seemed its inevitable consequence deprived NATO as well as the Warsaw Pact of their rationale.

At the end of some otherwise banal reflections on the Tiananmen Square massacre, the philosopher Norberto Bobbio quoted Kavafis's famous poem 'Waiting for the Barbarians', about an ancient city thrown into confusion when the expected invasion does not take place: 'what will become of us without barbarians?'[32] What indeed would become of NATO without the Evil Empire to justify its existence? One of the most piquant sights of 1989 was the evident lack of enthusiasm with which George Bush and his most loyal European ally, Margaret Thatcher, greeted an event which they had long demanded – the opening of the Berlin Wall – and the imminent attainment of a long-standing foreign-policy objective of their governments – the reunification of Germany. It was understandable enough that Gorbachev, while reluctantly ready *faute de mieux* to accept the effective collapse of the Warsaw Pact, should fight a rearguard action first against a united Germany and then against its inclusion in the Western alliance. These were rational, if doomed, attempts to salvage something from the wreckage. But there was something very remarkable about the vehemence with which Mrs Thatcher – the Iron Lady herself – repeatedly described not just NATO but the Warsaw Pact as forces for 'peace' and 'stability' in Europe. There could be no clearer indication of the mutual dependence of the two blocs.

One major theme of Washington's response to the upheavals in Eastern Europe was an effort to ensure a continued role for NATO and therefore for the US in Europe. Secretary of State James Baker chose Berlin for the venue of a major speech in December 1989 that called for 'a new architecture for a new era' central to which was what the *Financial Times* called 'the conversion of NATO into a more general alliance which, while still dealing with security issues, would increasingly concern itself with political and economic relations with the Soviet Union and Eastern Europe'.[33] At much the same time defence analyst Lawrence Freedman argued that it would be in the West's interest if the Warsaw Pact were to survive and play 'a more political role', thereby becoming 'the critical mechanism for preventing the fragmentation of Eastern Europe', and the 'enormous strains' which 'social, economic and political upheavals in the East' would place on Western Europe.[34] The fact remained, however, that, as Ian Davidson pointed out, 'NATO military doctrines are in tatters', since 'the political transformations now taking place in Eastern Europe completely undermine the political acceptability of a doctrine which assumes the use of nuclear weapons against East Germany, Czechoslovakia or Poland.'[35] Indeed, the negotiations between NATO and the Warsaw Pact aimed at reducing Russian and American troop levels in Europe conjured up what Davidson called the 'unsettling prospect of a superpower-free Europe' implying a variety of scenarios ranging from the collapse of NATO to the emergence of 'a united Europe with a significant arsenal of its own nuclear weapons'.[36]

Whatever the precise outcome, it was clear enough that Kennedy's 'multipolar world' was in the process of emerging. One factor favouring this development was a discernible trend, to some extent qualifying the more sweeping claims about the tendency of capital to become globally mobile, towards a certain regionalization of economic relationships. West Germany's influence as a trading economy was highly concentrated in Europe: in 1988 54.4 per cent of West German exports went to the rest of the EC, 16.7 per cent to the European Free Trade Association, and 5.6 per cent to the main Eastern bloc economies.[37] This pattern was likely, if anything, to be reinforced by the greater integration of the EC and the opening up of Eastern Europe. A North American trade bloc might emerge with the extension of the US–Canada Free Trade Agreement to include Mexico. The boom in the Pacific Rim economies during the late 1980s was to a significant extent a reflection of the growing involvement of Japan in the region. The *Financial Times* reported in early 1990 that 'Japanese companies are building a commercial empire in east Asia.' The surge in Japanese direct investment in East Asia – it rose from $1.4 billion in 1985 to $5.6 billion in the year to March 1989, dwarfing US direct investment in the region of $2.3 billion in 1988 – was in large part a response to the rise of the yen in late 1985. Japanese multinationals in search of lower labour costs quickly expanded operations especially in such 'second-wave' NICs as Thailand, Indonesia, and Malaysia. Trade also grew: long the largest exporter to East Asia, Japan began rapidly to increase its imports from the region – up 20 per cent in 1989 alone.[38]

The Bush administration's plans to reduce US military strength in the Pacific would, together with Japan's growing economic involvement in East Asia, encourage Tokyo to assume a larger military role in the region. Japanese defence spending, though still restricted to between 1.0 and 1.6 per cent of gross national product (depending on the estimates used), already added up to a formidable total: in 1988 the Japanese military budget was the third largest in the world. That year the Melbourne *Age* reported on Tokyo's plans for the expansion of the 'Self-Defence Force':

Japan's navy is the fourth biggest, in terms of tonnage. Within two years Japan will have more tactical aircraft than the US has defending continental America. It will have three times as many destroyers as the US Pacific Fleet, and five times as many Orion patrol aircraft.[39]

These trends conjure up the image of a state-system in which Japan and Germany compete on terms of complete equality with the US and the USSR, former superpowers come down in the world – a view implicit, for example, in André Gunder Frank's *bon mot*: 'The Cold War is over. Japan and Germany won it.'[40] Matters are not, however, so simple. The US in fact enjoyed a number of significant victories in the 1980s. Washington contained any new revolutionary challenges in the Third World and adopted, under the name of the Reagan Doctrine, what Fred Halliday calls 'a policy of counter-revolution on the cheap', involving especially the promotion of right-wing guerilla movements against various Moscow-aligned regimes (Nicaragua, Angola, Cambodia, Afghanistan).[41] In 1987–8 US military intervention on the side of Iraq secured Iran's defeat in the Gulf war, offering some revenge for the humiliations of the 1978–9 Revolution and the subsequent seizure of the American embassy in Tehran.

The disintegration of the Russian empire in the short term further strengthened Washington's hand in the Third World. Indeed, the timing of the successful American invasion of Panama in December 1989, only weeks after the East German and Czechoslovak Revolutions, no doubt reflected the Bush administration's sense of the greater room for manoeuvre open to the US thanks to Moscow's retreat in the Third World and preoccupation with the unfolding domestic crisis. The invasion itself gave the lie to Western apologists such as Ash who seek to present the US as a state whose behaviour towards its dependants is morally superior to that of the USSR. According to Panamanian church and civil rights organizations, some 3,000 civilians died in the invasion, more than ten times the official US estimates. (Other estimates range as high as 7,000.) Mass graves were discovered containing corpses with hands tied behind their backs, and others incinerated with flame throwers. Alexander Cockburn commented:

Anyone wearying of announcements that the cold war is over should study closely what has happened in Panama, and understand that the cold war, as actually fought by the US against the third world, i.e. the war the US took seriously, beyond posturing about the Soviet 'threat' to keep military appropriations at full tilt, is as before, and, indeed, is intensifying.[42]

The pretext for the invasion – the Noriega regime's involvement in the drug trade – indicated one way in which continued US intervention abroad could be justified. The moral panic against drugs had already been used in support of a higher level of repression within the US itself – for example, paramilitary police sweeps through the black ghettos of Los Angeles. Perhaps it would also become a standard defence for the assertion of US hegemony in Latin America – one might call it 'narco-imperialism' – now that invocations of the Evil Empire were no longer credible.

These developments, in conjunction with the East European revolutions, might seem to license the conclusion that the world had entered an era, not of 'multipolarity' but of renewed US dominance. Halliday argues that

> there is only one 'superpower', the USA. The USSR has lost its leverage in Europe, with the collapse of the Warsaw Treaty Organization, is weakened and preoccupied by economic and social crisis, and is not able to compete with the USA or the West more generally in the military and economic spheres. The USSR is now little more than a continental power, without a supportive alliance system. The illusion of 'rough parity', as Brezhnev liked to call it, is no longer sustainable.[43]

The prospect, on this argument, is of US 'ultra-imperialism', unchallenged by any major rival. But surely this goes too far. For one thing, the USSR, though shorn of the outer rim of its empire in Eastern Europe, will remain a major industrial and military power – so long as the government in Moscow does not lose control of the economically crucial Ukraine, linchpin of the Russian state since the seventeenth century. For another, the contradiction between America's global politico-military hegemony – undoubtedly reinforced by the immediate impact of the East European revolutions – and its relative economic decline has not been abolished by the partial disintegration of the Russian empire. Indeed, the developments discussed earlier, by encouraging the greater political assertiveness of the German and Japanese ruling classes, are likely to exacerbate this contradiction. And the opening of the Berlin Wall will not somehow magically abolish Washington's twin deficits. The Cold War turned out to be a long slugging match between two heavyweights. In the last round, the weaker has collapsed under the punishment he suffered, but the battered victor stands reeling over him, eyeing the new contenders waiting outside the ring.

Whether Japan and a German-dominated EC eventually translate their economic power into comparable military strength depends on a variety of imponderables – for example, the course of European political integration. What is not in doubt is that the world at the end of the twentieth century increasingly resembles its condition at the beginning of the same century. Then a number of Great Powers – Britain, Germany, the US, France, Austria–Hungary, Russia, Japan – competed for influence. They were not on equal footing: Britain, centre of the world system since the Napoleonic wars, was still what *1066 and All That* would call Top Nation, though its position was being eroded by the development of major industrial economies in the US and Germany. The rise and decline of powers, combined with the potential for shifting alliances created by the existence of a *plurality* of major states, tended to destabilize the world system. Similar uncertainty seems likely to be the world's fate at the turn of the twentieth century. The partition of the globe between the two superpowers and their allies and dependants was restrictive and oppressive in innumerable ways. It meant, however, that world politics was reasonably predictable, despite the constant danger that the arms race would get out of control. The erosion of superpower dominance and the re-emergence of a multipolar world make for a much less predictable state of affairs; the existence of several major power-centres recreates the conditions for alignments that cut across the old blocs and rearrange themselves when states' perceptions of their interests change. There thus takes shape again the minuet of Great-Power competition which before 1939 in Europe led often to 'diplomatic revolutions' and sometimes to war.

The illusion that the end of the Cold War marked the beginning of an era of global stability and peace, whether under a renewed American hegemony or a superpower condominium, was in any case rapidly dispelled. The crisis unleashed by the Iraqi invasion of Kuwait in August 1990 underlined both the extent and the limits of change. One important development in the 1970s and 1980s had been the emergence of regional powers in the Third World, aspiring to the kind of local dominance enjoyed by the superpowers on a far larger scale. The causes were various, and included the industrialization of parts of the Third World and the American policy, formalized in the 1970 Nixon Doctrine, of encouraging friendly regimes (Israel, Iran, Brazil, South Africa) to act as 'subimperialisms' defending Western interests in strategically important areas. The effect was to introduce into certain regions the same kind of economic and strategic competition between heavily armed powers which on a global scale precipitated the two world wars and sustained the Cold War – for example, the

successive conflicts between India and Pakistan, the simmering rivalries between Turkey and Greece, and the Gulf war between Iran and
Iraq of 1980–8. The last of these clashes, costing over a million lives,
indicated the limits of these subimperialisms' autonomy of the Great
Powers: Iraq's victory depended, as we have seen, on the intervention
of a US determined to contain, and, if possible, reverse the Iranian
Revolution.

The same factors were at work in the summer of 1990: Saddam
Hussein's attempt to solve Iraq's economic crisis and consolidate its
regional dominance by seizing Kuwait brought him into direct
conflict with the Western powers. The speed and scale of the
American response did not simply reflect the strategic importance of
the oil sheikhdoms for the Western economy. Washington's room for
manoeuvre had been greatly increased by the removal of any inhibi-
tion on military intervention in the Middle East for fear of unleashing
a superpower confrontation: Moscow's effective withdrawal from the
region and support for international action against Iraq had eliminated that threat. But it was also likely that the Bush administration
seized on this new crisis as an opportune occasion to reassert US
hegemony in the West. The enormous American military build-up in
the Gulf was a salutary reminder to Tokyo and Bonn – Helmut Kohl
only weeks earlier had offended Washington by securing Soviet
agreement to reunified Germany's membership of NATO through
bilateral negotiations with Gorbachev – that the security of their oil
supplies still depended ultimately on the Pentagon. Some took
comfort from the virtual unanimity with which the United Nations
authorized action against Iraq. But this was less a sign of the renewed
authority as a peacemaker of a body that had allowed flagrant
aggressions to go unpunished as recently as the American invasion of
Panama than an indication of the consensus temporarily prevailing
among the Great Powers. The world was still one in which imperialist
states were willing to go to war to preserve their control of strategic
portions of the globe – though the military strength accumulated by
Iraq showed how far some ex-colonies had been able to rise above
mere client status. The hazards and uncertainties of the Gulf crisis
underlined that what was taking shape after the Cold War was not a
new world order but a more dangerous version of the old.

3.2   THE GREAT ILLUSION

The potentially destabilizing consequences of the East European revolutions were sufficiently obvious to encourage widespread discussion of possible mechanisms for containing them. Perhaps the most popular remedy was the further development, in both depth and extent, of the European Community. Faster movement towards a federal Europe, already on the agenda because of discussions within the EC to supplement the Single European Market due to be established in 1992 with economic and monetary union, would help to limit the disruptive impact of German reunification by, as Kohl put it, 'provid[ing] the Germans with a more solid European roof'.[44] At the same time, the post-Stalinist governments in Eastern Europe generally pressed for incorporation in the EC. This was not simply in the hope that West European prosperity would, as a result, rub off on them but because of a belief in the special political virtues attached to the EC states. Precisely what these virtues consisted in was a matter of some controversy, but it was quite widely felt that the EC represented a social-democratic variant of liberal capitalism which offered a better model than the *laissez faire* extremes of the New Right governments in the US and Britain. Interviewed a year before the East European revolutions, the French Prime Minister, Michel Rocard, described himself as a keen 'European federalist' and argued that '[w]hat sets Europe apart is not just its high level of economic development, nor its political pluralism, but its systems of social protection.'[45] Opponents of closer EC integration such as Mrs Thatcher and her supporters objected especially to the commitments to state intervention and welfare measures embodied in the Community's Social Charter. They seized on the prospect of a wider EC embracing the former Stalinist regimes in the East to argue against further integration, but other governments, notably the French, found wider support when they pressed for economic, monetary, and political union as the most appropriate response to the 1989 revolutions.

Very striking in all this were the positive connotations attached to the concept of Europe itself, not simply in the EC and the newly emancipated countries to its east, but also in the USSR. Gorbachev's invocation of a 'common European home' was echoed even by one of his sternest left-wing critics, Boris Kagarlitsky, who called Marxism 'the path to European civilization'.[46] But it was East European intellectuals who brought out most explicitly the salient cultural and political assumptions involved in this foregrounding of the idea of Europe. Thus in 1983 the Czech novelist Milan Kundera wrote an evocative elegy for Central Europe – those countries, notably Czechoslovakia, Hungary, and Poland, which, part of the Russian,

German and (especially) Austro-Hungarian empires before 1914, when they were the centres of a brilliant Modernist culture, enjoyed a brief period of independence between the wars, before once again being subjected to alien rule, this time from Moscow. This political subordination was, Kundera argued, a cultural exclusion from Europe:

> In fact, what does Europe mean to a Hungarian, a Czech, a Pole? Their nations have always belonged to the part of Europe rooted in Roman Christianity. They have participated in every period of its history. For them, the word 'Europe' does not represent a phenomenon of geography but a spiritual notion synonymous with the word 'West'.

Hence the threat to the very identity of Central Europe, 'a condensed version of Europe itself in all its cultural variety', arising from its subjection to Russia, 'uniform, standardizing, centralizing', not 'one more European power' but 'a singular civilization, an *other* civilization' characterized by a 'terrifying foreignness'.[47]

It does not make one an apologist for Russia's postwar empire to find much of Kundera's argument absurd. Critics were, for example, bemused by the affection he displayed for the Austro-Hungarian empire, despite the systematic denial of national rights especially to Slavs on which it was based.[48] There was, moreover, something profoundly impoverished morally about a historical vision which seemed able to imagine the European culture of the past two centuries without – merely to mention some Russian writers – Pushkin, Gogol, Turgenev, Dostoevsky, Tolstoy, Mayakovsky, Bulgakov, Babel, Pasternak, and Solzhenitsyn. In a brilliant *aperçu* C. L. R. James observed that the great nineteenth-century Russian writers 'are as distinct a stage of the European *consciousness* as was, in its way, the Classical Philosophy, and they deserve a place in a new *Phenomenology of Mind*'.[49] But some of the most gifted East European intellectuals are now eager to write Russia out of the story. Even a writer as normally indulgent to their vagaries as Tim Garton Ash noted of two of them, Václav Havel and György Konrad, that they 'use the terms *Eastern Europe* or *East European* when the context is neutral or negative; when they write *Central* or *East Central*, the statement is invariably positive, affirmative, or downright sentimental'. Ash underlines 'the mythopoeic tendency' involved in such distinctions: 'We are to understand that what was *truly* Central European was always Western, rational, humanistic, democratic, sceptical and tolerant. The rest was East European, Russian or possibly German.'[50]

It is clear enough that involved here is an exercise in ideology rather than historical analysis. Even Jenö Szücs's serious and scholarly effort to characterize East-Central Europe as a historically distinct region, intermediate between the West and Russia, respectively identified by István Bibo with 'motion' and 'immobility' arising from the former's separation and the latter's fusion of state and civil society, is careful to isolate several markedly different variants, in particular those represented by the Polish-Lithuanian aristocratic republic, Prussian absolutism, and the Habsburg realms.[51] And *Mitteleuropa* in what Kundera believes to be its heyday before 1914 displayed in a concentrated form many of the characteristic ailments of the twentieth century: it was, after all, in its greatest city, Vienna, that, under the mayorship of Karl Lüger, anti-Semitism first became a form of sustained popular mobilization.[52] Ash reports François Bondy's 'telling ... riposte to Kundera': 'if Kafka was a child of Central Europe, so too was Adolf Hitler.'[53]

Facts are, in any case, beside the point in what is essentially a political discourse. Europe, as Eric Hobsbawm shrewdly observed, is 'a continent whose very definition has been political'.[54] The point of the vogue for *Mitteleuropa* is both to include Russia out as a centre of Asiatic barbarism and to revalue Europe as a civilization embodying the highest political and cultural values. The argument is spelled out by Mihály Vajda, who treats 'Europe' as 'a specific value system, a way of thinking, and during recent decades ... a political concept'. From this perspective 'Russia is *not* Europe', but 'a world system going its own sweet way', which 'involves rejection of all the ideas essential to what we call European civilization: its value system, its ways of thought, its concepts of freedom and of the individual'. Vajda argues that '[t]he non-existence of autonomy – indeed the lack of even a *desire* for autonomy – is the main distinguishing feature of Eastern Europe, in contrast to Europe proper.'[55]

There is, in fact, something quite monstrous about the one-sidedly positive identification of Europe with the 'concepts of freedom and of the individual' that has become typical of contemporary discourse. This complex of ideas is associated with another currently fashionable notion, that of 'cultural heritage'. The resulting amalgam is well summarized in Gorbachev's reference to 'a deep, profoundly intelligent and inherently humane European culture'.[56] Now carrying on a tradition necessarily involves a process of selection from the past, but the sheer humbug involved in contemporary conceptions of Europe was never better exposed than by Walter Benjamin in his masterly reflections on the whole subject of tradition. Discussing the notion of 'cultural treasures', he wrote:

> a historical materialist views them with cautious detachment. For without exception the cultural treasures he surveys have an origin which we cannot contemplate without horror. They owe their existence not only to the great minds and talents who have created them, but also to the anonymous toil of their contemporaries. There is no document of civilization which is not at the same time a document of barbarism.[57]

And – as Benjamin was all too aware when he wrote these lines in 1939, when the prospect of Europe was far darker than it would seem fifty years later – there is no continent fuller of documents of barbarism than Europe. The continent which produced the *Mona Lisa* and Mozart also sheltered Auschwitz and Treblinka. The Nazi extermination camps were, after all, the creation of the culturally and economically most advanced nation of Europe. It was perhaps indicative of the same politico-intellectual climate that produced the kind of persuasive redefinition of Europe given by Kundera, Vajda et al. that the West German intelligentsia should be divided in the late 1980s by a debate – the *Historikerstreit* – the two sides to which sought to explain away Nazism either as a pale copy of the Stalinist terror or as a consequence of the archaic, premodern character of German society. Both cases were apologetic in effect if not (at least in the case of those such as Jürgen Habermas who rejected Ernst Nolte's claim that the Holocaust was merely a variation on a 'Bolshevik' theme as an attempt to rehabilitate German nationalism) in intention, since neither recognized fascism for what it was – the offspring of a crisis of advanced capitalism, whose conditions, although especially acute in Weimar Germany, could be repeated, with potentially similar consequences. Nazism was not an aberration from European modernity but a product of its deepest strains.[58]

That Nazism is as much a part of the European 'heritage' as the concept of individual freedom is confirmed by reflection on the historical process through which this continent came by the nineteenth century to dominate the rest of the globe. The two world wars were after all the culmination of a succession of relentless military struggles among the Great Powers inseparably connected with the development of the world market and the formation and extension of capitalist relations of production. One of the main dimensions of this process – the political and economic subjugation of the other continents to the West European powers and their Russian and North American extensions – ensured that conflicts within the European state system exacted a terrible price from the peoples of Africa, Asia, and Latin America. It is thus impossible to separate Europe's achievements from the horrors it has wreaked on humanity. Perhaps the most beautiful room I have ever been in is the Codrington Library in All Souls College, Oxford, which was built with the profits of the slave trade.

Maybe all this can now be forgotten in the prosperous liberal democracies of the contemporary EC. Matters are not, however, so simple. Geoffrey Barraclough, surveying the history of attempts at European unity, notes that 'it proved far easier, when it came to defining what constituted Europe, to formulate a negative, exclusive notion of European unity directed against some allegedly non-European or anti-European power or movement, than to find some pan-European objective to which all could adhere.'[59] The exclusion of Russia from Europe in the contemporary cult of *Mitteleuropa* is one example of this tendency. The drive to exclude is indeed a central feature of any discourse on Europe. The concept of Europe acquired currency in the early-modern era as a substitute for the mediaeval notion of Christendom, which had become the self-description of one of the two main successor civilizations to the Roman empire. The other, Islam, also defined itself in religious terms. In the Middle Ages, Judith Herrin observes, '[r]eligion had fused the political, social, and cultural into self-contained systems, separated by their differences of faith.'[60] In the sixteenth and seventeenth centuries, however, 'Christendom' was increasingly supplanted by 'Europe', a more secular concept shorn of Christianity's (potentially) universal aspirations and identified with what Fernand Braudel would call a distinct 'world economy', the European state-system then in the process of expanding into the rest of the globe.[61] Europe, however, continued to define itself through its antagonistic relationship to an Other – in the early-modern era the contemporary embodiment of Islam in the very threatening shape of the Ottoman empire. More generally, as Edward Said shows in his splendid philippic against Orientalism, Europe's sense of its own identity has depended on the supposed existence of an opposite, the East, passive, static, despotic, and sensual where the West is active, dynamic, free, and rational.[62] The persistent tendency (even by radical Soviet intellectuals) to portray Russia as an Asiatic despotism inserts itself all too easily into this discourse.

The potentially racist implications of this conception based on both exclusion and asserted superiority should be plain enough. Thus

Orientalism easily adapted itself to the biological race theories of nineteenth-century social Darwinists and proto-fascists.[63] The experience of the Nazis (who were, incidentally, rather free with their invocations of European civilization) has made explicit appeal to these theories disreputable, but the same ideological assumptions persist, usually lurking behind a discourse of 'cultural difference'.[64] The main precipitant of contemporary racism is, of course, the constant recomposition of the Western working class by waves of Third World immigrants. The issues posed by this process highlight the problematic nature of the present cult of Europe. Where do the millions of descendants of Europe's colonial or semi-colonial subjects now living in the EC – Indians, Algerians, Turks, Bangladeshis, Indonesians, Pakistanis, Afro-Caribbeans, Vietnamese – fit into Kundera's 'Europe rooted in Roman Christianity'?

The current reactivation of traditional pathological fears of Islam – a product largely of the Iranian Revolution and the associated rise of Islamic fundamentalism as a challenge to Western interests – carries with it profound dangers of racial polarization given that Western Europe now has a substantial Muslim minority. Anti-Muslim hysteria, which the Rushdie affair showed to extend well beyond the far right to much of the liberal intelligentsia, can feed into a more general paranoia, in which Europe together with what Kagarlitsky calls its 'post-European' extensions in the US and USSR, sees itself threatened by a rising tide of archaic irrationalism.[65] The most likely beneficiaries would be the home-grown irrationalists of the European extreme right. The 1980s saw not merely the imposition of tighter immigration controls by European governments of all political colours but the electoral growth of parties whose main plank was anti-immigrant racism – the Front National in France, the Republikaner in West Germany, the Progress Party in Norway. The use of Salman Rushdie's name by white youths who would otherwise have detested his politics, his colour, and (were they, most improbably, to read them) his novels as a racist taunt aimed at British Asians is an indication of the contorted character of cultural politics in contemporary Europe.

The upshot of all this is not that anyone who espouses the 'European idea' is somehow a closet racist. It is rather that the current vogue for sanitized versions of the European 'heritage' both obscures the problematic and contradictory character of that heritage (the difficulty is precisely that so many documents of barbarism are *also* documents of civilization: if this were not the case then outright rejection would be more appropriate than Benjamin's 'cautious detachment') and potentially colludes – especially in the anti-Islamic revival – with full-blown racism. In any case, the belief that a sense of European identity provides the means for defusing the destabilizing consequences of the collapse of Stalinism is an illusion. Politically, this sense of identity can take various expressions. One is a federal European state, a project only remotely plausible in anything like the short or medium term in the current EC: I consider it below. Another is the much older idea of what Barraclough calls 'unity in diversity' – de Gaulle's 'Europe des patries' taken up by Mrs Thatcher in her campaign against EC integration, a community of nation-states sharing a common culture and co-operating politically and economically but remaining legally sovereign.[66] The disintegration of the Russian empire is likely to boost this latter conception of Europe. For East Europeans, appeal to the 'European idea' has involved, not simply the demand for liberal-democratic freedoms, but also the assertion of national self-determination. The claim of Poland, Czechoslovakia, Lithuania, or the Ukraine to be an old European nation, whether real or spurious, serves to legitimitize the demand for national independence.

Neal Ascherson, for many years an eloquent promoter of this dialectic between a wider European identity and national demands, has emphasized the fissiparous consequences it is likely to have in the wake of the 1989 revolutions:

> Europe is a patchwork of tensions. Some, though persistent, are harmless. Some may have great destructive power, deriving from historic hatreds. In the West, these sores are generally in the open. In the 'ex-Soviet zone' of Europe, they have been sealed off by taboo for 40 years and nobody knows how much of their venom they will retain when the seals are broken.[67]

Many of these potential conflicts – Ascherson counted forty-six national grievances and border disputes involving European states – arose from the legitimate demand for self-determination by oppressed peoples, notably in the case of the various subject nationalities in the USSR: Russia's possessions in the Transcaucasus and Central Asia, mainly the Romanovs' conquests in the eighteenth and nineteenth centuries, were after all the last of the old European colonial empires. But even here, as the conflict between Armenia and Azerbaijan over Nagorno-Karabakh indicated, legitimate independence movements could be deflected into ferocious inter-ethnic conflicts (no doubt with some encouragement from Moscow: Jerry Hough argues that the rise of nationalism in the various Soviet republics was one of Gorbachev's strongest cards, both because of the divisions among the nationalities and the Russian chauvinist reaction unleashed by their demands[68]). Elsewhere the collapse of Stalinism helped political movements to gain office by stirring up appalling atavistic hatreds: in April 1990 elections swept to power both the Hungarian Democratic Forum, a party all too ready to play on anti-Semitism and on dreams of restoring Hungary's pre-1919 borders at the expense of Czechoslovakia, Romania, and Yugoslavia, and Croatian nationalists enjoying the backing of veterans of the wartime pro-Nazi Ustashe and benefiting from the backlash created by the aggressive Serbian expansionism espoused by the Stalinist regime of Slobodan Milošević. *Old* Europe, the Europe whose power-struggles and national conflicts twice pitched the world into war, is back from the grave.

One of the many paradoxes of the East European revolutions was that they thus strengthened (and perhaps helped to proliferate) the nation-state as the main form of political community in the modern world at the very time when the internationalization of capital was undermining its economic power. This contradiction between global economic integration and the nation-state was indeed one main factor involved in the proposals further to integrate the EC. Agreement to establish a Single European Market by 1992 and the project of economic, monetary, and political union were in large part a response to the belief, widely shared by the Western ruling classes in the 1980s, that the EC found itself in a weak competitive position relative to the US and Japan. Indeed, until the upheavals of 1989 transformed the standing of Germany, a main theme of Reaganite and Thatcherite propaganda was the 'stagnation' to which the 'corporatist' Bundesrepublik was supposedly doomed. A far more rational appraisal of the EC's common plight was expressed by Paul Kennedy, who argues that '[i]n its *potential*, the EEC clearly has the size, the wealth, and the productive capacity of a Great Power', whose combined GNP would allow it to match the military establishments of the superpowers. 'And yet', he continues, 'Europe's real power and effectiveness in the world is much less than the crude total of its economic and military strength would suggest – simply because of disunity.'[69]

Concern about Western Europe's apparent technological disadvantage compared to the US and Japan, about its lack of a unified domestic market, about the need for the assertive use of state power in the growing conflicts over trade among the major Western economies, about the apparent shift from the Atlantic to the Pacific as the main axis of the world system helped to create the political basis for proposals to transform the EC from a common market to a politico-economic unit possessing some of the features of a federal state. Even conflicts among the major West European states contributed to this process. Thus the Franco-Italian desire to participate in control of the European Monetary System, effectively dominated by the West German Bundesbank, helped to produce the Delors report of April 1989, which contained the radical proposal for 'a *transfer of decision-making power* from member-states to the Community as a whole ... in the fields of monetary policy and macroeconomic management' – a move, if implemented, which would mark the first real step from a confederal association of states to a European federal state.[70] Fears about the disruptive impact of German reunification have also, as we have seen, encouraged calls to accelerate the process of political and economic union.

It is a moot point whether the East European revolutions will actually speed up or delay EC integration. Much depends on whether the absorption of East Germany, in altering the priorities and boosting the self-confidence of the West German ruling class, causes serious damage to the Bonn–Paris axis that has been the linchpin of the EC since the time of Adenauer and de Gaulle. What is certain is that, contrary to the illusions entertained with extraordinary naïvety by the new governments in Eastern Europe, the existing EC will be extremely reluctant to add to the already serious problems created by the economic gulf separating northern from southern Europe by incorporating the impoverished and unstable successors of the Stalinist regimes. The doors of the Community will not be speedily opened to embrace Eastern Europe (except, of course, for the special case of East Germany). In any case, even assuming that the conflicts of interest among the West European states were overcome and a more federal though geographically narrow EC were established, it is not clear how this would contribute to remedying the problems diagnosed in the first part of this chapter. Preparations for the Single European Market give some indication of the likely outcome of further EC integration. Employers in the richer parts of the Community sought to use the imminent abolition of intra-European trade barriers to demand that their workers accept reductions in wages and conditions to levels closer to those in the poorer Mediterranean countries: the incorporation of eighteen million skilled but (by north-European standards) low-paid East Germans would add to these pressures. Externally, though the more extreme North American and East Asian fears of a protectionist 'Fortress Europe' might prove exaggerated, a stronger, more unified EC would conduct itself more aggressively within a Western bloc increasingly riven by trade disputes. And the reduced military presence of the superpowers in the continent would inevitably lead to a greater strategic role for Western Europe – a development to some extent foreshadowed by greater European involvement under the aegis of NATO in the Mediterranean and by France's activities in the Indian Ocean. A stronger EC would contribute to, rather than help contain, the global anarchy.

Beliefs to the contrary, on the left at least, rest on the idea, mentioned at the beginning of this section, of the 'European model' of socially regulated capitalism which provides an alternative to the unfettered free-market capitalism of the New Right. Thus Paul Hirst writes:

> The most successful industrial economies in the modern world – Japan and West Germany, Northern Italy and Sweden – have not favoured an economic free-for-all. They have in contrast pursued strategies of economic co-ordination, regional regulation, and co-operation between industry, labour, and the state. In Italy and Japan, particularly at the regional level, such strategies have helped to compensate for the failings of their national political systems. Britain and the US have set their face against such strategies, failing to see the economic benefits of a more collaborative political culture and prizing, above all, the sovereignty of the market and the right of management to manage without check.[71]

The difficulty with this kind of contrast is that, for one thing, it overstates the difference between the 'Anglo-Saxon' and 'Euro-Japanese' models. As we saw in the previous section, state intervention in the economy, including the use of classic Keynesian demand-management techniques, remained a central feature of *all* the advanced capitalist countries in the 1980s, whatever the political colour of their governments. There were indeed significant differences in the form taken by this intervention, but to assimilate the roles of such very different state agencies as, say, the Japanese Ministry of International Trade and Industry and the West German Bundesbank to a common pattern responsible for relative economic success involves a gross and misleading oversimplification. Secondly, a static comparison of supposedly different 'models' leaves out of account the *direction* of economic policy in the 1980s and 1990s. As John Grahl and Paul Teague rightly observe, the Single European Market marks the 'culmination' of a 'neo-liberal advance' in which

> the drive towards a renewed subordination of workforces has found

unity and direction in the demand for *labour flexibility*, while deregulation, trade-union reform, tax reductions, have worked to widen the field of action for business enterprises, now revalued socially and culturally to become not only indispensable instruments of economic progress but even privileged sources of value and meaning.[72]

Any attempt to identify European social democracy as the political bearer of an economic alternative to *laissez faire* founders on the central role played by the parties of the Second International in this 'neo-liberal advance'. With a handful of exceptions (Kohl, Genscher, Thatcher) the key West European political figures of the 1980s and early 1990s have been social-democrats – Mitterrand, González, Craxi, Palme, Papandreou. The record of 'Eurosocialism' in office has been uniformly grim. Some have not even made obeisances towards the idea of an alternative to neo-liberalism: thus González in Spain was content to draw the political dividends deriving from his role in constructing a stable post-Franco regime. Papandreou, after similarly benefiting from measures of social modernization, following PASOK's election in 1981, implemented in 1985 Thatcherite austerity measures which precipitated the fiercest social conflicts of the decade in the West. The most important social-democratic government in the continent, and the only one to attempt extensive nationalization and counter-cyclical economic policies, the Mitterrand administration in France, changed course in 1983 as a result of a massive flight of capital and the pressures exerted on the franc through the West German-dominated European Monetary System.

By 1990 'Mitterrand, the monetarist' was receiving the rather sardonic praise of the *Financial Times*, which compared him favourably with Mrs Thatcher for having 'pursued a single-minded disinflationary policy' after 1983:

The contrasts with the UK are remarkable. In what started off as Mr Mitterrand's Keynesian France, broad money grew by 53 per cent between 1983 and 1989; over the same period, it grew by 142 per cent in Mrs Thatcher's supposedly monetarist Britain. Mr Mitterrand's Socialist Government allowed real wages to rise by less than 6 per cent between 1983 and 1989, while Mrs Thatcher's allegedly harsh treatment of organized labour produced real wage increases of 20 per cent. Under Mr Mitterrand the unemployment rate rose from 8.3 per cent in 1983, to a peak of 10.4 per cent in 1987, and was still 9.4 per cent in February 1990. Under Mrs Thatcher, the unemployment rate peaked at 11.4 per cent in 1986, but fell quite sharply, to 6.1 per cent in February 1990.[73]

Nor was there much comfort to be gained by looking outside the EC to Austria and Sweden, those strongholds of neutralist social democracy which supposedly had been able to avoid the neo-liberal rigours imposed elsewhere. The late 1980s saw a large-scale reorganization of Austrian capitalism involving in particular the contraction and subjection to much harsher market disciplines of the state-owned Austrian Industries. The East European revolutions and their aftermath distracted attention from the virtual disintegration of the Carlsson government in Sweden after both employers and unions vetoed a proposed wage-freeze in February 1990. The effective collapse of Swedish 'corporatism', which had involved systematic collaboration between (usually social-democratic) governments, big business, and trade-union bureaucracy, came amid a wave of strikes and lock-outs and against the background of a worsening economic crisis. Its main features – a projected balance of payments deficit of nearly £4 billion in 1990, prices and unit labour costs rising at twice the Western average, economic growth the second lowest in the OECD – were more reminiscent of Mrs Thatcher's Britain at the end of the 1980s than Hirst's inclusion of Sweden among 'the most successful industrial economies in the modern world' would lead one to expect.[74]

Rather than embodying any distinctive pattern of development, Western Europe at the beginning of the 1990s thus seemed to be experiencing the same process that had cracked open the Stalinist states, what Chris Harman has called the 'transition from national to multinational capitalism'. Neither nation-states nor the proto-federal state which the EC might become represented any real framework for containing and controlling the operations of the world market, whose power seemed to grow by the year. Is there really no alternative to this almighty market?

4

BEYOND THE MARKET

'Down with Communism.'
Graffito on a Bucharest wall, February 1990, underneath which was
written in another hand:

'What is this phenomenon? We have never experienced it!'

4.1 THE NECESSITY OF PLANNING

Absurdly, though perhaps not surprisingly, much of the left now believes that there is no alternative to the market as a basis for running an advanced economy. This profound political and intellectual shift gained pace throughout the 1980s. Its Bible was Alec Nove's *The Economics of Feasible Socialism* (1983). His insistence that any workable socialist programme must rely on market mechanisms was taken up by a group of British intellectuals, organized under the aegis, ironically enough, of that old citadel of statism, the Fabian Society, but enjoying official encouragement from Neil Kinnock's New Model Labour Party. This group – among them David Miller, Raymond Plant, and Julian Le Grand – sought to construct models of 'market socialism'.[1] But many of the original East European proponents of this idea which had been fashionable during the era of economic reform in the 1960s, now seemed to have settled for the market *tout court*. Włodzimierz Brus, for example, apparently reduces the role of socialism in the formula merely to a set of values promoting the humane management of market economies.[2] Even the new left emerging amid the ruins of Stalinism seemed sometimes to countenance the idea that greater reliance on market mechanisms would mark an economic advance in the USSR and Eastern Europe.[3]

The vogue for the market was understandable enough in some respects. After all, both the Stalinist and the social-democratic left identified socialism with state control of the economy. The Stalinist bureaucratic command economy represented the most extreme form taken by the left's statism, but even right-wing social-democratic opponents of extensive nationalization such as Anthony Crosland tended to equate socialism with state direction of the national economy by means of Keynesian demand-management techniques. The economic crises of the 1970s and early 1980s demonstrated the severe limits of national economic management in the era of multinational capitalism: the collapse of the Mitterrand administration's left-Keynesian economic programme in 1981–3 was probably the most dramatic episode in this process. The advanced economies' recovery from the 1979–82 recession, when counterposed with the stagnation of the Stalinist bloc, served further to underline the apparent strength and relative efficiency of liberal capitalism. The East European revolutions could only serve to reinforce the same conclusion, that, in Tim Garton Ash's words, 'there is no "socialist economics", there is only economics. And economics means not a socialist market economy, but a social market economy.'[4]

The left's enthusiasm for the market is thus not all that surprising, given its previous statism. It is still absurd, though this is usually concealed by the theoretical terms on which market and planned economies are compared. Nove's presentation of the argument is typical: despite his protestations to the contrary, it essentially involves counterposing an idealized model of the market found nowhere outside neo-classical textbooks to 'really existing socialism' – i.e., the Stalinist bureaucratic command economy. Nove's actual case for the market is in no sense original. It largely echoes the arguments of neo-liberal economists such as Ludwig von Mises, Lionel Robbins, and Friedrich von Hayek in the immediate aftermath of the October Revolution. They contended that a planned socialist economy cannot solve the problem of rationally allocating resources to different uses. Choosing the best use of a given resource depends on being able to calculate the costs and benefits involved in various alternatives. Market prices, reflecting the supply and demand of goods and services, provide the necessary information: they allow the capitalist to determine the most profitable employment of the resources at his command. Socialism, by suppressing prices and money, which make it possible to treat all goods and services as substitutable for one another, destroys this system of calculation without replacing it with another. Mises concluded: 'Every step that takes us away from private ownership of the means of production and from the use of money also takes us away from rational economics' and towards 'recourse . . . to the senseless output of an absurd apparatus'.[5]

This argument did not go unchallenged when it was first put

forward between the wars. Thus Fred Taylor and Oskar Lange showed how allocative efficiency could be achieved in a planned economy where there still existed a market for labour-power and consumer goods but not for investment goods.[6] Nove, however, is concerned less with any such comparison of theoretical models than with an attempt to demonstrate the superior allocative efficiency of the market over planning through a detailed discussion of the irrationalities of the Stalinist command economy. His argument boils down to three points. First, the suppression of the market in a complex modern economy necessarily leads to the construction of centralized bureaucratic structures in order to co-ordinate the vast range of productive activities undertaken by any such economy: 'The elimination of commodity production, with production for use and not for exchange, implies a degree of centralization which has a multilevel, hierarchically organized plan-bureaucracy as its functionally inescapable accompaniment.' Secondly, 'most of the major problems now plaguing the Soviet economy . . . arise directly or indirectly out of the *vast scale and innumerable interdependencies* of the modern industrial economy.' The inability of the central planners to process the vast quantities of information required for them to perform their task gives rise to the chaotic struggle of ministries and enterprises. Thirdly, the only alternative to this system is offered by a market economy. 'In a complex industrial economy the interrelation between its parts can be based in principle either on freely negotiated contracts, or on a system of binding instructions from head office. There is no third way.' And the market, by offering a set of competitively formed prices reflecting the distribution of supply and demand, represents a form of organization which is both more efficient and more democratic than planning.[7]

Nove's arguments have been subjected to detailed and convincing criticism, notably by Chris Harman and Ernest Mandel.[8] I do not intend to repeat their arguments in any great detail. But it cannot be stressed sufficiently how loaded Nove's comparison between planned and market economies is. On the one hand, Nove claims that a planned economy must necessarily take the form of the Stalinist bureaucratic command system. But in what sense can the Stalinist economies be described as planned at all? In the classical Marxist tradition, planning is understood as the allocation of resources on the basis of decisions taken collectively and democratically by the associated producers. Marx believed that such a system of *ex ante* allocation, in which decisions about the use of resources seek to anticipate and shape the development of the economy as a whole,

rather than react *ex post* to the signals provided by the fluctuation of
prices in response to changes of supply and demand, would realize
two goods among others: consumption would become the goal of
production, rather than the self-expansion of capital, while the direct
producers would be able collectively to determine their fate, to be
autonomous, in a sense denied them under capitalism.

Now it is plain enough that the Stalinist system in no way resembles
such a planned economy. This is not simply because of the authoritarian, profoundly undemocratic character of the bureaucratic command economy. As we saw in chapter 3, consumption – even the
consumption of the bureaucracy – cannot be described as the goal of
an economy skewed massively in the direction of the production of
investment goods. The goal of capitalism – production for production's sake, as Marx put it – seems rather to prevail. Nor can this set
of economic priorities be plausibly regarded as an outcome freely
chosen by planners or Politburo. It is rather a consequence of the
competitive pressures which, since the late 1920s, have compelled the
Soviet regime to give priority to the heavy industries on which the
USSR's military position relative to the West depends. The kinds of
irrationalities and inefficiencies on which Nove dwells – and which
had been diagnosed long before by Marxists such as Cliff and
Harman – arise from the highly centralized system of vertical controls
erected in the 1930s to solve the problem of how to mobilize the
resources needed in a backward and isolated economy to build the
industrial base of military strength.[9] To insist in this way on the need
to understand the historical context in which the bureaucratic
command economy emerged is in no way to deny or seek to excuse
the innumerable crimes and idiocies involved in creating and sustain-
ing this system. It is, however, to challenge the idea that the Stalinist
system is a variant (indeed, if Nove is right, the only historically
practically realizable variant) of socialist planning. 'Really existing
socialism' is (increasingly, was) a variant of *capitalism*, in which
global military competition compelled the subordination of production within the USSR to the goal of capital accumulation.

Equally misleading is the other term of Nove's comparison. Contemporary market economies bear little resemblance to the competitive models of neo-classical textbooks. 'Really existing capitalism' is
characterized by the extreme centralization of economic power, the
dominant role played by huge corporations organized increasingly
across international borders. Within these corporations the market is
effectively supplanted as a means of co-ordinating economic activities
by bureaucratic structures of control in principle identical to those

prevailing in the Stalinist economies. Nove indeed acknowledges the importance of 'large corporations, within which the links are those of subordination–coordination, i.e. vertical and not (or as well as) horizontal'.[10] But he does not face up to a major consequence of the development of these structures, namely that, as Harman puts it, 'internal waste and inefficiency proliferate while success in holding on to markets for decades at a time is often accompanied by neglect of innovation and deliberately allowing poor quality production': the American car industry during the postwar boom is a classic case in point.[11] As this example indicates, firms which respond to their domination of the market in this way are likely eventually to become vulnerable to the competition of new, more efficient rivals: in the 1970s Nemesis arrived in Detroit in the shape of the great Japanese car firms. But this is hardly grounds for celebrating the virtues of the market in the manner of Nove and his co-thinkers, whether neo-liberal or social-democrat. For, in the first place, the impact of competition tends to make itself felt less in the shape of a process of continuous adjustment through which the less efficient firms reorganize themselves and adopt more productive techniques, but catastrophically, with the destruction or drastic contraction of entire sectors. (One of the major faults of neo-classical economics, with its emphasis on marginal alterations, is that it underplays the extent to which change involves qualitative transformation rather than gradual adjustments.) Productive resources – workers, machinery, and the like – consequently go unused. This form of waste, inherent in market economies, tends to give rise to state intervention, which seeks to prevent the collapse of uncompetitive sectors, at the price of impeding the kind of reorganization required to achieve substantial increases in productivity. The Western response to the October 1987 stock market crash shows the extent to which state manipulation of the market has survived the intellectual collapse of Keynesian economics (see section 3.1 above). Non-market forms of co-ordination, and the forms of waste and inefficiency they entail, are endemic to 'really existing capitalism'.

These arguments do not amount to the claim that Western capitalism is more inefficient than, or even as inefficient as, the Stalinist economies. As we saw in chapter 2, the global integration of capital, most fully realized in the West, has put the bureaucratic state-capitalist economies of the East at an increasing disadvantage. But the collapse of one variant of the dominant mode of production should not obscure the extent to which contemporary multinational capitalism still has many of the features of the statized, 'organized' economies of the era of national capitalism. Nor does the economic bankruptcy of Stalinism imply that the market – to which the internationalization of capital has given greater scope – provides the best framework in which the left should seek to improve the human condition. On the contrary, the classical Marxist critique of the market, and of the capitalist system from which it is indissociable, retains all its force.

This critique makes three main claims against the market economy: that it gives rise to *exploitation*, that it is *anarchic*, and that it makes human beings *unfree*. It is worth briefly stating the contemporary relevance of each of these claims. It is, in the first place, the cornerstone of Marx's *Capital* that a system of generalized commodity production, where labour-power itself has become a commodity purchased and sold on the market, necessarily involves the exploitation of labour. The theorists of the New Right have directed much of their fire against this idea, but to little effect. Robert Nozick, for example, seeks to depict capitalism as a society in which differences of wealth and income reflect transactions voluntarily undertaken by free citizens. But, quite aside from the flaws internal to his argument, this picture seems simply absurd when set beside the reality of contemporary capitalism, with the vast concentrations of economic power represented by bureaucratically managed corporations.[12] It was of course precisely the inequality of power between the capitalist, controlling the productive resources of society, and the worker, owning nothing but her labour-power, which Marx identified as the basis of capitalist exploitation.

How do market socialists respond to Marx's theory of exploitation? David Miller argues that a market economy is not necessarily exploitive. On the contrary, 'there are no deep conceptual grounds for thinking that markets cannot allocate resources in accordance with personal deserts' and indeed 'there are good positive reasons for taking equilibrium prices as indicators of value when measuring desert'. Lest anyone blench at the idea that the earnings of, say, a nurse and a stockbroker represent their relative worth, Miller hastens to explain that the kind of market which will produce a just outcome is one which has been 'given an appropriate regulative framework'; this framework seems to involve, in particular, eliminating the 'asymmetries in bargaining power' between capital and labour which, Miller concedes, give rise to exploitation. Miller's non-exploitive market is, in other words, not the kind of market that we find in 'really existing capitalism', but an idealized one from which the feature responsible for exploitation has been removed. To show that such a market is either feasible or desirable would require establishing two propositions at least: first, that Marx was wrong when he made one of his best-established predictions, namely that market competition involves a tendency towards the centralization and concentration of capital which has produced the kind of economy under which we live today; secondly, that, assuming that Miller's idealized market could be organized, it would have positive virtues which make it worth attaining. Miller makes no attempt to defend the first proposition, but does claim various virtues for markets, notably that 'they are the best known means of ensuring that consumers get what they want.'[13]

This assertion involves a pretty heroic idealization by comparison with the actuality of the market economy at the beginning of the 1990s. Most of the Third World has suffered grievously in the past decade: the debt crisis in particular has served as a mechanism for transferring wealth from the poor to the rich countries (see section 3.1 above). Famine repeatedly struck Africa, though not, as latter-day followers of Malthus would have us believe, because of a tendency for the growth of population to outstrip that of food production. On the contrary, as Anatole Kaletsky wrote at the height of the Ethiopian famine of 1984–5,

> In the world as a whole, there is now more food per head than ever before in history, and food production is likely to go on rising faster than population for the rest of the century – cereals production will increase by 2.5 to 3.5 per cent a year, against worldwide population growth of 1.7 per cent a year, between 1980 and 2000 according to World Bank, US Agriculture Department and UN Food and Agricultural Organization (FAO) projections. Even the poorest developing countries, as a group, have increased their per capita food production substantially since 1960 and will, on present trends, make even greater strides by the year 2000. In the short term, of course, huge surpluses of cereals and dairy products are being stored in government silos and refrigerated butter mountains all over America and Europe.

Africans starve not because of an absolute scarcity of food but because of what Amartya Sen calls a failure of entitlements – crudely put, the poor's lack of the money required to buy the food available in abundance on a world scale. This situation is a consequence of what Kaletsky describes as 'an unprecedented financial and economic crisis' involving 'a vicious pincer movement of rising food prices, falling commodity prices and declining aid'. By 1984 Africa's foreign debt represented 58 per cent of GNP compared to Latin America's 46 per cent. It was Africa's poverty, arising from its position within the world market, which bred famine.[14]

Nor is poverty confined to the periphery of the system. The 1980s saw social and economic inequalities widen in the advanced economies, especially in those countries such as the US and Britain where New Right governments cut income tax for the rich and social-security payments for the poor. By 1988 there were nearly 32 million people below the official poverty line in the US, compared to about $24\frac{1}{2}$ million a decade earlier – an increase from $11\frac{1}{2}$ per cent to just over 13 per cent of the population. The growth of poverty reflected a redistribution within American society from poor to rich. The House Ways and Means Committee estimates that the top five per cent of US families increased their share of pre-tax income from 21.4 to 26.2 per cent in 1980–90, while the share of the bottom 20 per cent fell from 4.5 to 3.7 per cent. Nor was this merely a relative change: the top fifth of American families had seen their real incomes rise by 31.7 per cent, while the bottom fifth were 3.2 per cent worse off.[15] Similar policies under Mrs Thatcher in Britain have produced dramatic rises in the levels of poverty and homelessness and a perceptible 'Americanization' of social life, reflected for example in Cardboard City, the wretched encampment of street people alongside the theatres and museums of London's South Bank. The consequent rise in social tensions created the climate in which the biggest British riot for over a century took place in Trafalgar Square on 31 March 1990 at the end of a demonstration against the local government poll tax, a measure which brought into focus the government's efforts to take from the poor and give to the rich.

If the market as it actually exists really is 'the best known means of ensuring that consumers get what they want', then the future of humankind is likely to be grim indeed. Marx argued that the systematic socio-economic inequalities characteristic of the contemporary world were constantly reproduced by capitalist exploitation. There seems to be no good reason for believing him to have been mistaken. But Marx did not simply condemn capitalism because it is founded on class exploitation. He regarded it as the most dynamic of class-based modes of production. Its two most basic features – the exploitation of wage-labour and competition between capitals – make possible an enormous expansion of the productive forces under capitalism. At the same time, however, these very features mean that humanity does not fully benefit from the productive potential created by capitalism. The case of famine mentioned above offers an illustration: their vulnerable position within the world market explains why many Africans live on the edge of starvation even though technical progress has enabled food production to outstrip population growth. Capitalist relations of production, which tie people's access to resources to the money they possess, mean that the development of the productive forces does not lead to a corresponding increase in well-being.

This conflict between the forces and relations of production is most pronounced in respect of the anarchic character of capitalism. Competition between capitals is an inherent feature of this mode of production, though the form it takes has varied according to the stage of capitalist development and as the agents of competition have themselves changed – from the family firms of the Victorian era, through the militarized state capitals of the first half of this century, to the multinational corporations of the present. In all these phases capitalism has involved the absence of any overall regulation of production: the allocation of resources to different sectors of the economy has been the outcome of a competitive struggle in which each capital has looked to its own self-expansion rather than the stable development of the system as a whole. Consequently, as Marx put it, 'a balance is in itself an accident owing to the spontaneous nature of this production.'[16] Not simply may the supply of and demand for a specific good fail to correspond, but *generalized* market failure, in which an overall imbalance of supply and demand occurs, is a possibility inherent in capitalism by virtue of the fragmented and *ex post* nature of decision-making inherent in commodity production. Such situations are, of course, much more than abstract possibilities. The history of capitalism has been regulated by the oscillations of boom and slump, in which the disequilibria of supply and demand created by competition have been corrected by generalized recessions. The process highlights the waste endemic to the market economy, since balance is restored in recessions through allowing productive resources – workers, machinery, buildings, and land – to go unused until the consequent fall in their prices makes resumed production and new investments profitable. The movement of capitalist development takes a spiral form, in which output and productivity tend in the long term to rise, but the trend is punctuated by crises exacting a heavy toll in human misery and lost production.

The history of capitalism also comprises efforts to impose some form of social regulation on the anarchy of the market. The rise at the beginning of the twentieth century of what Hilferding called 'organized capitalism' seemed to offer these efforts their best hope: not only were markets increasingly manipulated by large firms but private capital itself tended to become integrated with the nation-state. But a degree of regulation within the boundaries of nation-states was bought at the price of global anarchy, as the militarized state capitals sought to carve out the globe between them. And the long period of economic expansion which followed the last partition, at the end of the Second World War, promoted an internationalization of capital which has severely reduced such economic power as the nation-state possessed. The world has entered in the past twenty years a far more 'disorganized' era, as the flows of capital and commodities escape national control.[17] As we saw in chapter 3 above, these changes have been part of the more general move of the world economy into a new era of instability. Inasmuch as the East European revolutions contribute to the reduction in state economic regulation, they will promote the development of 'disorganized capitalism'. The result may be some phases of very fast growth, but they are likely to be accompanied by equally deep recessions. A less regulated world economy may well be one characterized by the kind of roller-coaster of sharp booms and slumps that was a chronic feature of capitalism before the Second World War.

Capitalism is not, however, merely exploitive and anarchic; it denies human beings control over their own lives. Defenders of the market tend to prize it as the bearer of individual freedom by virtue of the greater scope for choice it offers economic actors. Now Marx did not simply dismiss these claims out of hand. He recognized that the ability of workers to choose between employers and to some extent to shape their consumption according to personal tastes by their purchases was one of the respects in which capitalism represented progress by comparison with earlier modes of production such as slavery and feudalism.[18] Nevertheless, he insisted on the *formal* character of freedom under capitalism: above all, the worker's lack of access to productive resources other than labour-power compel her to accept employment on terms that involve her exploitation. Once again, there seems little reason to alter this judgement. Apologists for the market make much of 'consumer choice'. But, in the first place, consumers' ability to purchase goods depends on their income, which in turn reflects their position in the labour-market. The widespread poverty in the advanced countries, evidence of which I cited above, means that the choice of many is very heavily constrained by the low wages or social-security benefits they receive. But, secondly, the alternatives open even to the better-paid are limited by the domination of Western retail markets by a few big corporations. In Britain, for example, five companies accounted for 74 per cent of packaged grocery sales in

1988, and, if present trends continue, three supermarket chains will dominate three-quarters of food retailing by 1995.[19] The development of 'niche markets' directed especially at upper-income consumers during the recovery of the 1980s encouraged the belief that mass markets were breaking up, but the reality seems more to be the emergence of new retail chains, so that Benetton and the Body Shop take their place alongside Safeway and Marks and Spencer. The globalization of capital brings in its wake a further standardization of consumption patterns, of which the arrival of McDonald's in Moscow seems an apt symbol.

But capitalism does not simply offer individual freedom subject to strict limits: it systematically impedes the attainment of autonomy, by which I mean human beings' collective control over their lives. The fragmentation of social experience under capitalism encourages individuals to see their personal lives as the only source of meaning. The 'process of personalization' analysed by Gilles Lipovetsky, the way in which consumer choices acquire central importance as they come to involve the selection of a lifestyle in which the person's very identity is involved, is one symptom of the intense emotional investment of private life under contemporary capitalism, and its obverse, the draining of meaning from the public world.[20] But it is not just that this condition corresponds to what Marx called alienation, since human beings are unable to realize themselves through a shared engagement in the world. It is also that the lack of autonomy places us in circumstances of direct and increasing danger.

The tendency for the consequences of human actions to outdistance their initiators' expectations is greatly strengthened by the fragmented and anarchic character of capitalist production. Thus Marx explained the liability of the rate of profit to fall in terms of the ultimately self-defeating efforts of individual capitals to increase their profits by introducing labour-saving innovations.[21] In recent years, however, it has become clear that the uncontrolled development of the productive forces is causing unexpected and potentially catastrophic damage to the earth. The most important of these effects are, of course, the growing evidence of global warming as a result of the accumulation of carbon dioxide and other gases in the atmosphere and the destruction of the ozone layer by chlorofluorocarbons and other industrially produced chemicals. The likely outcome is hard to predict, since highly complex interactions between various forces and processes are involved, but some scientists refuse to rule out rapid and drastic climatic changes bringing in their wake very widespread devastation.[22] Avoiding disaster – perhaps the destruction of humankind – requires the mobilization of resources on a global scale. It is simply inconceivable that the efforts needed, for example, to plant trees and reduce carbon emissions on the scale required to reverse global warming can be organized within the framework of the market. It is, after all, the competitive pursuit of profit that is the prime cause of environmental destruction. The threat, for example, to the Amazon rainforest comes from an array of social forces – land speculators, cattle ranchers, rubber barons, and landless peasants – whose struggles reflect the wider contradictions of Brazilian capitalism.[23] The possibility of catastrophic climatic change highlights the conflict between the need for global co-operation to achieve a rational management of the environment and the prevailing organization of the world into competing states and firms. Our lack of autonomy is not merely a moral evil but a mortal danger.

Capitalism thus stands condemned. A different form of society is required which would eliminate exploitation, overcome the anarchy inherent in capitalism, and achieve the kind of collectively regulated relationship to our natural environment without which humankind may perish. Marx believed that these requirements would be fulfilled by communism, the rule of the associated producers. I discuss some of the features of this type of society in section 4.3 below, returning there to some of the claims made for the market. Let us first, however, consider the political framework in which capitalism can be removed.

4.2 SOCIALIST VERSUS LIBERAL DEMOCRACY

It is now platitudinous to associate socialism and democracy. After Stalinism, everyone on the left agrees, socialism can only advance if it assumes a democratic form. But 'democracy' is usually equated here with a specific institutional form, that of modern liberal democracy. Some remarks of Agnes Heller's are fairly representative. What she calls 'the "formal" character of modern democracies' is essential – the 'relative (never complete) separation of state from society' and 'a fundamental document (mostly in the form of a constitution) which formulates the democratic civic liberties, pluralism, the system of contract, and the principle of representation'. Heller identifies this 'formal democracy' with democracy as such. Indeed: 'All those who want to replace formal democracy with so-called substantive democracy, and thereby reunify state and society in a totalizing way, surrender democracy as such.' Displaying the intolerance which, alas, all too often is shared by both perpetrators and victims of Stalinism,

Heller therefore proposes to exclude from the left all those unwilling to pursue socialist objectives 'within the framework of formal democracy'.[24]

Heller's stress on the separation of society from the state highlights a leitmotif of opposition thought in Eastern Europe which has come to have some influence on the Western left, namely the concept of civil society. Tim Garton Ash calls 1989 'the springtime of societies aspiring to be civil'.[25] Indeed, dissident intellectuals in Poland began in the late 1970s to describe themselves, and later Solidarność, as representing the forces of 'civil society' in opposition to the state – a move which Z. A. Pelczynski rightly describes as 'a truly remarkable intellectual development. Few social and political concepts have travelled so far in their life and changed their meaning so much.'[26] The history of this concept has been traced by Norberto Bobbio, who distinguishes two decisive stages. First, Hegel identified civil society primarily with the economic relations of capitalist society, a move influenced by his reading of the classical political economists which determined Marx's usage of the term. Secondly, however, Gramsci, while still, like Hegel and Marx before him, counterposing civil society and the state, tended to identify the first term of the opposition with cultural and political institutions which were part (in Marxian terms) of the superstructure rather than of the economic base.[27] Thus, as Pelczynski puts it,

> Gramsci's civil society contains two indistinctly separated elements: a realm of independent social organizations and non-governmental institutions..., and a realm of what one might call, following Tocqueville, 'political society', existing outside and in opposition to the state, and made possible by a degree of social autonomy.[28]

The history packed into the concept of civil society lends it a certain ambiguity. This is tacitly acknowledged and indeed made a virtue of by one of its main Western promoters, John Keane:

> Modern civil societies have comprised a constellation of juxtaposed and changing elements that resist reduction to a common denominator, an essential core or generative first principle. They have included capitalist economies and households; social movements and voluntary public spheres (churches, organizations of professionals and independent communications media and cultural institutions); political parties, electoral associations and other 'gatekeepers' of the state–civil society distinction; as well as 'disciplinary' institutions such as schools, hospitals, asylums and prisons.[29]

It is not at all obvious why a democratic political life should depend on promoting *all* the elements of this highly heterogeneous list. Ash plays on the ambiguity of *bürgerlich*, which can be translated as either 'bourgeois' or 'civil', to equate the triumph of civil society with that of the market. 'Yes, Marx is right,' he has the peoples of Eastern Europe say, 'the two things are intimately connected – and we want both! Civil rights and property rights, economic freedom and political freedom, financial independence and intellectual independence, each supports the other.'[30] But anyone less gullible about the teachings of the New Right is unlikely thus to equate capitalism and democracy (an equation which those living outside Europe and North America are in any case much less tempted to make). Yet the concept of civil society seems to encourage precisely this kind of confusion. For that reason its use is an obstacle to serious discussion of the relationship between socialism and democracy.

For Heller the relationship is simple enough: 'formal democracy can be transformed into a socialist democracy without being altered one iota.'[31] An incomparably more realistic view of the relationship between liberal democracy and socialism is offered by Bobbio, who is at the same time the most lucid contemporary exponent of the idea that the former provides the sole appropriate framework in which the latter may be achieved:

In advanced capitalist societies, where economic power is becoming increasingly concentrated, despite universal suffrage, the formation of parties with a mass base and the reasonably high degree of political mobilization, democracy has not yet succeeded in keeping its own promises which principally centred on three objectives: (1) participation . . . ; (2) control from below . . . ; (3) freedom of dissent. In states where democratic institutions are more fully and formally developed, two phenomena have been shown to occur which militate against the declared principle of general participation: on the one hand political apathy, in other words a lack of participation (which is tacitly interpreted as an expression of the highest degree of consensus with the prevailing system); and on the other, participation which is distorted, deformed or manipulated by the entities that have the monopoly of ideological power over the masses. Control from below becomes progressively less effective as the centre of power shifts towards these entities, with the result that the institutions which the citizen succeeds in controlling are increasingly fictitious as centres of power. Meanwhile the various centres of real power of a modern state, such as big business, or the most significant *instruments* of real power, such as the army and bureaucracy, are not submitted to any democratic control. In fact it is possible to speak of an actual subsystem of political power, not in the sense that it comprises forces of a secondary order but because they are primary and yet cannot be seen: they are occulted. As for the right of dissent, this can only operate within a highly circumscribed sphere: within the dominant economic system which never offers the possibility of a radical alternative.[32]

This analysis draws Bobbio towards the conclusion that 'the democratic method as it is practised within a capitalist system does not seem to allow for the transformation of that system, i.e. the transition from a capitalist to a socialist society'. He elaborates the point by considering the dilemma facing any attempt to transform capitalism gradually by means of 'structural reforms':

> can the reform of a given mode of production be brought about by a series of piecemeal reforms, none of which is decisive? Let us assume that total transformation can result from a series of partial reforms: up to what point will the system be prepared to accept them? Can the possibility be excluded that there is a limit to the system's tolerance, so that a point is reached where the system can no longer bend, and so shatters? If those whose interests are threatened react violently, what is there to do except respond with violence?[33]

The picture Bobbio paints of 'really existing' liberal democracy is all the more telling since he is such a vehement opponent of any revolutionary challenge to this political order. The three main features he identifies find all too many illustrations in the contemporary West: *a passive citizenry* – in the 1988 presidential elections in the US, upper-income electors were twice as likely to vote as lower-income electors;[34] *the displacement of parliamentary institutions by unelected centres of power* – the *Spycatcher* and Wallace affairs brought into the public domain the role played by the British security services in the attempted destabilization of the 1974–9 Labour government and Mrs Thatcher's accession to the leadership of the Conservative Party; *structural constraints on the piecemeal transformation of capitalism* – it was above all the massive flight of capital from France which forced the Mitterrand administration to abandon the programme of reforms on which it was elected in 1981.

It is precisely because of the presence of these features that classical Marxism has insisted on describing liberal democracy as *bourgeois* democracy. This description is not equivalent to the dismissal of liberal democracy as a mere 'façade' whose replacement by, say, fascism or a military dictatorship should be a matter of indifference to socialists. On the contrary: Lenin and Luxemburg both argued that the left should strive to achieve bourgeois democracy as the capitalist political form providing the most favourable conditions for the development of the working-class movement; Trotsky in his classic writings on German fascism was equally emphatic that revolutionary Marxists should resist attacks on parliamentary institutions from the right.[35] Nevertheless the Marxist critics of liberal democracy insisted that it was not a neutral institutional framework consistent with socialism as well as capitalism, but a specific form of bourgeois class rule, one among a range of state-forms through which capitalist domination is secured.[36]

But is there a democratic alternative to liberal democracy? Bobbio thinks not, and consequently has in recent years moved in a liberal, indeed increasingly in a conservative, direction: faced with the choice between socialism and 'really existing' democracy, he opted for the latter, despite his realistic appreciation of its limitations.[37] But Bobbio provides only the most cursory of arguments to establish that parliamentary government is the only feasible form of democracy.[38] The historical record, in fact, contains several different kinds of democracy, involving particular institutional forms and legitimating ideologies, and embodying specific forms of class rule.[39] There is, of course, the classical case of the Athenian city-state of the fourth and fifth centuries BC: the forms of direct democracy developed there made possible a degree of participation in government by the direct producers of town and country unprecedented by modern liberal standards, although their control over slave-labour permitted the landed gentry to exercise ultimate (if contested) domination.[40] Of much more immediate relevance, however, is the rich twentieth-century tradition of soviet democracy, of workers' councils which develop into at least the embryo of a new form of political rule.

The most distinctive feature of the soviet as a political institution is that it is based not on any particular geographical unit, but on the workplace. It emerges from the process of production, and organizes the producers collectively. Typically, the soviet embraces all those employed in a particular workplace, cutting across the boundaries created by the division of labour, and those between different trade unions and indeed between trade unionists and unorganized workers. The soviet, furthermore, involves a distinctive combination of direct and representative democracy: decisions are taken by a body of delegates elected and subject to immediate recall by assemblies of workers in the different sections of the workplace. This delegate structure provides scope for the unification of workplace soviets into wider, geographically based workers' councils at a local and national level: thus Russia in 1917 saw the efflorescence of factory committees, district and city soviets, and regional and all-Russian congresses of soviets. Finally, soviets represent a tendency to break down the distinction between economics and politics characteristic of capitalist societies. Thus the original soviet was formed in St Petersburg in October 1905 when a strike by typesetters demanding a shorter working day and a higher piecework rate per 1,000 letters set, including punctuation marks, developed into a political general strike which forced the Tsar to concede a constitution; before the 1905 Revolution was finally defeated, the St Petersburg soviet had become, according to its president, Trotsky, 'a workers' government in embryo'.[41]

Trotsky later summarized the conditions under which soviets emerge:

> The soviets are created when the revolutionary movement of the working masses, even though still far from an armed insurrection, creates the need for a broad authoritative organization, capable of leading the economic and political struggles embracing simultaneously the different enterprises and the different trades.[42]

Soviets are thus not the conscious creation of a party or movement pursuing an explicit political project. On the contrary, as Lenin argued, the soviet 'is not anybody's invention. It *grows* out of the proletarian class struggle as that struggle becomes more widespread and intense.'[43] One of the most striking features of twentieth-century world politics is indeed the frequency with which soviet-type forms have developed in conditions of great working-class mobilization. The Russian Revolutions of 1905 and 1917 proved to be merely the beginning. The period of revolutionary instability throughout Western and Central Europe after the First World War saw the development of workers' councils, most notably the German *Rate* and the *commissioni interni* of Turin. The working-class reaction to Franco's coup in July 1936 created, especially in Barcelona, forms of popular self-rule which subverted the Republican government as well as challenged its fascist opponents. The climax of the Hungarian Revolution of 1956 was marked by the assumption of effective control by workers' councils. The domination of the factories by the French Communist Party meant that the great general strike of May–June 1968 threw up soviet-type forms only in a highly localized and sporadic way, but the universality of these forms was demonstrated most dramatically at the end of the 1970s. The decisive factor in the overthrow of the Shah of Iran in 1978–9 was a series of mass strikes which stimulated the development of factory councils, the workers' *shoras*; the establishment of the Islamic Republican Party's hegemony after the Revolution depended on the destruction of these *shoras*. Finally, Solidarność during its heyday in 1980–1 was more than a mere trade union, both in its class-wide, radically democratic forms of organization and in its aspiration to 'a Self-Managed Republic' under workers' control.[44]

Running like a red thread through the history of the twentieth century is thus the tendency of mass working-class struggles which go beyond purely economic demands and thereby at least tacitly challenge the power of the state to throw up organizational forms reflecting and asserting workers' collective strength in the process of production. Now the claim of classical Marxism is that these forms represent the basis of a new form of political power capable of supplanting the existing state and providing the framework for the transition to a classless communist society. Gramsci argued:

> The socialist state already exists potentially in the institutions of social life characteristic of the exploited working class. To link these institutions, co-ordinating and ordering them into a highly centralized hierarchy of competences and powers, while respecting the necessary autonomy and articulation of each, is to create a genuine workers' democracy here and now – a workers' democracy in effective and active opposition to the bourgeois State, and preparing to replace it here and now in all its effective functions of administering and controlling the national heritage.[45]

It is the initially spontaneous development of this molecular organization of workers' councils that, for the revolutionary socialist tradition, gives substance to Lenin's claim that the dictatorship of the proletariat involves 'an immense expansion of democracy, which *for the first time* becomes democracy for the poor, democracy for the people, and not democracy for the money-bags'.[46] For much of the left, however, the idea of a socialist democracy superior to liberal democracy has become a Utopian dream which perhaps harbours within it the nightmare of Stalinism. Persuasive arguments in support of this view are, nonetheless, hard to come by. One objection to soviet democracy is offered rather cursorily by Bobbio, who says that its theorists suffer from 'a refusal to believe that there are problems relating to the citizen distinct from those regarding the worker (or the producer)'.[47] This is a strange claim. Bobbio himself, as we saw above, notes as one of the structural defects of liberal democracy the absence of any kind of democratic control over the vast concentrations of economic power characteristic of modern capitalism. Nationalization is now generally acknowledged to offer, in itself, no remedy for this situation: state monopolies are no more democratically accountable than private ones. Soviets represent the highest form in which the only real 'countervailing power' to that of capital is mobilized: the organized strength which the working class develops at the point of production. At the same time soviets put to use the detailed practical knowledge which workers possess of the process of production and on which capitalist managers tacitly rely while seeking to fend off any challenge to their control and to repress the vast, largely untapped creativity of most of their employees.[48]

It is hard to see how the organization of a modern industrial economy could be democratized except through the establishment of workers' control. The belief that soviets can also form the basis of a socialist state does not imply, as Bobbio asserts, the dismissal of problems which exist outside work. Capitalism has in the course of the twentieth century universalized wage-labour to a far greater extent than was true at the time of the Russian Revolution. The increasing domination of most women's lives by work outside the home, as well as the industrialization of parts of the Third World are both signs of this continuing process of proletarianization, contrary to the decline of the working class alleged by many Western social theorists.[49] Soviets thus organize people on the basis of the social feature that unites them in the largest numbers – their situation as wage-labourers – and build on the collective power which workers tend to develop in response to their exploitation. The progressive atomization of social life under modern capitalism leaves the workplace as the *only* remaining focus of collectivity, unless one counts those forms of identity – nationality, religion, race – which act as the basis of usually reactionary political mobilization. The collective organization and political self-consciousness generated through soviets can then provide the basis on which the problems people face outside work can be addressed.

Most objections to soviets tend to concentrate on their supposed imperfections as a democratic form. Thus Tim Wolforth argues that the decline of the soviets after the October Revolution reflected the Bolsheviks' failure to understand that '[a]s long as centralized decision-making is imposed by the circumstances of counter-revolution, war or scarcity', representative democracy, in the sense of 'the direct election by universal suffrage and secret ballot, through the free competition of parties, of the highest decision-making body of the government', is 'absolutely essential to ensure the "extension of actual democratic" usages in post-capitalist society'.[50] David Held seems to have a similar argument in mind when he suggests: 'it could be argued that, if one considers the problems of holding delegates at national level strictly accountable, the Commune system [i.e. soviets] might be better described as a highly *indirect* form of democracy.'[51] If the thought here is that parliamentary institutions are the most effective way of making the executive accountable to citizens, then proponents of this view must explain why these institutions so thoroughly fail to fulfil this role in modern liberal democracy. The insulation of the state bureaucracy from parliamentary supervision is one of the commonplaces of twentieth-century political science. Why should parliamentary institutions, so ineffective under capitalism, be the *sine qua non* of democratic accountability under socialism?

There are several respects in which soviet democracy would achieve a more genuine form of accountability than its parliamentary counterpart. For one thing, soviets imply the continuous and active involvement of citizens in government. Liberal democracy rests on a passive and atomized electorate which, on those relatively rare occasions when it is invited to express an opinion on who should govern it, is subject to a massive propaganda bombardment from media usually directly controlled by capital. Soviet democracy, by contrast, is based on a small unit organizing people collectively within the framework of a pervasive feature of everyday life – the workplace. Particularly given the tendency of soviets to develop spontaneously from mass working-class action, soviet democracy would in all likelihood involve a considerable decentralization of power to the smallest unit. And the counterpart to the system of delegation to higher bodies would be the right of lower bodies immediately to recall their delegates. This right was used to great effect to replace Bolshevik with Menshevik delegates to the Petrograd soviet after Red Guards had fired on demonstrators supporting the Constituent Assembly in January 1918.[52]

It was indeed the institution of a right of immediate recall, along with the suppression of the standing army and police, on which Marx seized when arguing that the Paris Commune of 1871 represented 'the political form at last discovered under which to work out the economical emancipation of Labour':

> While the merely repressive organs of the old governmental power were to be amputated, its legitimate functions were to be wrested from

an authority usurping pre-eminence over society itself, and restored to the responsible agents of society. Instead of deciding once in three or six years which member of the ruling class was to misrepresent the people in Parliament, universal suffrage was to serve the people, constituted in Communes, as individual suffrage serves every other employer in search for the workmen and managers in his business. And it is well known that companies, like individuals, in matters of real business generally know how to put the right man in the right place, and, if they for once make a mistake, to redress it promptly.[53]

The exercise of the right of citizens to exert continuous control over higher bodies by recalling unsatisfactory delegates would, however, be nullified in the absence of what Wolforth calls 'the free competition of parties'. Indeed, many critics of soviet democracy argue that Marxism's explanation of political conflicts in terms of class struggle and its inference that communism will involve the end of politics requires a monolithic one-party state. Held offers one version of this line of thought:

> After the revolution, there is a marked danger that there can only be one genuine form of 'politics': for there are no longer any justified grounds for fundamental disagreement. The end of class means the end of any legitimate basis for disputes: only classes have irreconcilable interests. It is hard to resist the view that implicit in this position is a propensity to an authoritarian form of politics. There is no longer a place for systematically encouraging and tolerating disagreement and debate on public matters. There is no longer a site for the institutional promotion, through the formation of groups and parties, of opposing positions. There is no longer scope for the mobilization of competing views.[54]

I consider whether communism would indeed be a society without difference and conflict in section 4.3 below. It is, however, essential to stress here that it is no part of classical Marxism to conceive of the dictatorship of the proletariat (understood in this tradition as the transitional phase between capitalism and communism) as involving the suppression of all parties other than that one held to represent the interests of the working class. Trotsky commented on Stalin's attempt to justify the CPSU's monopoly of power on the grounds that '[w]here there are not several classes, there cannot be several parties, for a party is part of a class' in terms that read like a direct response to Held's argument:

> It appears from this that classes are homogeneous; that the boundaries of classes are outlined sharply; that the consciousness of a class strictly

corresponds to its place in society. The Marxist teaching of the class nature of the party is thus turned into a caricature. The dynamic of political consciousness is excluded from the historical process in the interests of administrative order. In reality classes are heterogeneous; they are torn by inner antagonisms, and arrive at the solution of common problems no otherwise than through an inner struggle of tendencies, groups and parties. It is possible, with certain qualifications, to concede that 'a party is part of a class'. But since a class has many 'parts' – some look forward and some back – one and the same class may create several parties. For the same reason one party may rest upon parts of different classes. An example of only one party corresponding to one class is not to be found in the whole course of political history – provided, of course, you do not take the police appearance for the reality.[55]

The norm of soviet democracy is thus the free competition of parties. This follows indeed from the character of soviets as organs of the working class *as a whole*, their composition determined by the vote of workers or their delegates. Soviets are therefore multiparty organizations, and the suppression in Russia after the October Revolution of all parties except the Bolsheviks and indeed of factions within the ruling party was a sign of what Lenin himself called the regime's 'bureaucratic distortion'. Critics of soviet democracy, however, seize on this deviation of Bolshevik practice from Marxist theory in order to argue that 'the prohibition of opposition parties' was not, as Trotsky argued, 'a temporary evil', a 'measure dictated by conditions of civil war, blockade, intervention and famine', but was rather an inevitable consequence of the overthrow of parliamentary institutions leading ineluctably to Stalinism.[56] Interpretations of this kind typically identify the Bolsheviks' decision to disperse the Constituent Assembly in January 1918 as the turning point which set them on the road to the Gulag. This episode in fact raises several complex questions. One concerns the extent to which the Constituent Assembly elections, which gave the Social Revolutionaries (SRs) a majority of seats and left the Bolsheviks with only a quarter of the vote, accurately reflected the balance of social and political forces in a rapidly changing situation.[57]

There is, however, a more fundamental issue. The Constituent Assembly and the soviets were based on two fundamentally different systems of representation – respectively, the parliamentary form typical of modern liberal democracy, and the workplace-based delegate democracy discussed above. Each system of representation, and the assemblies issuing from them, embodied competing claims to democratic legitimacy and therefore constituted rival centres, or potential centres, of power. The Bolsheviks' decision to disperse the Constituent Assembly was mirrored by the Right SRs' and Mensheviks' intention to use their majority in the Assembly to reverse the outcome of the October Revolution. Marcel Liebman comments: 'In the last analysis, what causes surprise is not that Lenin assumed the responsibility of dissolving the Constituent Assembly, but that he took so long in deciding to do this, and had such difficulty in identifying the terms in which the dilemma – for there was a dilemma – presented itself, namely: Constituent Assembly *or* soviets.'[58]

This dilemma was ultimately one between two kinds of democracy that were incompatible because their institutional forms and legitimating ideologies involve two different systems of class power. The circumstances of the Russian Revolution presented this conflict in an especially acute form, since the numerical predominance of the peasantry gave the Bolsheviks' opponents a popular base, though one they squandered because of the Whites' insistence on restoring the land to the gentry. Nevertheless, the dilemma of bourgeois or proletarian democracy has reappeared in many later situations – for example, during the German Revolution of 1918 and the Portuguese Revolution of 1974–5. Liebman puts it thus: 'When we think of the great social clashes of modern times, we observe ... that the revolutionary dynamic has always been blocked by the paralysing or braking force of the electoral mechanism, even in its democratic form of universal suffrage.'[59] More precisely, when the radicalization of working-class struggles leads to the appearance, perhaps only in embryonic form, of soviet power, then parliamentary institutions tend to become the focus for counter-revolutionary forces, providing them with a means of democratically legitimizing the suppression of the revolution. The alliance of German Social-Democrats and proto-Nazi *Freikorps* under the banner of the Weimar assembly in 1919 is a classic example of this kind of polarization. Those such as Wolforth who seek somehow to marry parliament and soviets are simply seeking to evade the 'irrepressible conflict' of two kinds of democracy.

To opt, in this struggle, for socialist rather than liberal democracy is not thereby to reject what are sometimes called the classical 'liberal freedoms' – of speech, assembly, and association in particular. The belief to the contrary involves confusing these rights with certain institutional forms, namely those of liberal democracy. In fact, the liberal freedoms originated in the early-modern struggle against absolutism in the seventeenth and eighteenth centuries. It is a commonplace that the defenders of these rights in no way associated them with democracy in its ancient or modern senses. The liberal freedoms were intended to provide a space in which the citizen could pursue his goals independently of government; to the extent that the appropriate form of government came to be thought of as one based on parliamentary institutions, their electorate was initially confined to a small minority of propertied men. There is no reason to believe that socialist democracy, based as it is on the direct participation in government by the working masses through the agency of soviets, should not take over these freedoms and indeed, as Lenin and Luxemburg argued, greatly extend them by abolishing the disabilities arising from capitalist exploitation – for example, the enormous restrictions on freedom of speech arising from the fact that the mass media are dominated by the corporate rich.[60] Indeed, we have seen how the proper operation of soviet democracy depends on freedom of association.

The experience of capitalist democracy shows, however, that the relationship between democratic institutions and liberal freedoms is a complex one. Liberal democracies have, when their survival appeared to be threatened, been willing to make considerable inroads into civil rights. British governments during both world wars introduced detention without trial and extensive censorship. No socialist democracy could eschew similar measures of self-defence, particularly given the conditions in which it would, in all likelihood, come to power, as a result of revolutionary upheaval and in the face of external capitalist pressures. As is shown by the crises of liberal democracy, whether the use of exceptional measures against opposition by a revolutionary regime led to the kind of degeneration which followed October 1917 would depend on the strength of the institutions of soviet democracy, their ability to weather the vicissitudes of their situation. The experience of the Russian Revolution suggests that two factors in particular would be decisive – the size and socio-economic weight of the working class and the success of the revolution in spreading beyond its initial borders. There are in the nature of politics no guarantees that such a regime would survive and expand, but the incomparably greater development and integration of capitalism since the October Revolution create a far more favourable context than that which confronted the Bolsheviks.

4.3   TOWARDS COMMUNISM

Socialist revolution is conceived within the classical Marxist tradition as a political transformation – the overthrow of the existing state and its replacement by the rule of the workers' councils. But this episode, decisive though it is in (as Marx put it) 'converting the state from an organ superimposed on society into one completely subordinate to it', represents merely the beginning of a much longer and more far-reaching process of transformation.[61] Marx described the dictatorship of the proletariat, which he identified with the radically democratic forms of the Paris Commune, as 'no more than the transition to the *abolition of all classes* and to a classless society'.[62] The construction of a communist society is understood within the revolutionary tradition as a process, involving different phases to which particular measures are appropriate. Thus in 'The Critique of the Gotha Programme' Marx distinguished between lower and higher phases of communism: during the lower (the dictatorship of the proletariat), the social product will be distributed according to the principle 'from each according to his capacity, to each according to his works'; the inequalities to which this will give rise, since individuals differ in both their commitments and their endowments, would be remedied in 'a higher phase of communist society', where both the greater development of the productive forces and the transformation of personal motivations would make possible the application of a new distributive principle: 'From each according to his abilities, to each according to his needs!'[63]

The classical Marxist conception of the transition to communism as a long-term process of gradual transformation is fundamentally at odds with the millenarian and voluntarist fantasies of an immediate leap into a classless society which prevailed at the height of the 'Stalin revolution' in 1928–31 (see section 2.1 above). The exiled Trotsky was the firmest contemporary critic of these fantasies. The following passage from 'The Soviet Economy in Danger', written in October 1932, merits quotation at length, both because it anticipates currently fashionable critiques of the Stalinist bureaucratic command economy such as Nove's by half a century, and because it illustrates the belief – common to both Lenin and Trotsky – that the transition to communism would embrace a continued reliance on market mechanisms:

> If a universal mind existed, of the kind that projected itself into the scientific fancy of Laplace – a mind that could register simultaneously all the processes of nature and society, that could measure the dynamics of their motion, that could forecast the results of their interreactions – such a mind, of course, could *a priori* draw up a faultless and exhaustive economic plan, beginning with the number of

acres of wheat down to the last button for a vest. The bureaucracy often imagines that just such a mind is at its disposal; that is why it so easily frees itself from the control of the market and of Soviet democracy. But, in reality, the bureaucracy errs frightfully in its estimate of its spiritual resources. In its projections it is necessarily obliged, in actual performance, to depend on the proportions (and with equal justice one may say the disproportions) it has inherited from capitalist Russia, upon the data of the economic structure of contemporary capitalist nations, and finally upon the experience of successes and mistakes of the Soviet economy itself. But even the most correct combination of all these elements will allow only a most imperfect framework of a plan, not more.

The innumerable living participants in the economy, state and private, collective and individual, must serve notice of their needs and of their relative strength not only through the statistical determinations of plan commissions but by the direct pressure of supply and demand. The plan is checked and, to a considerable degree, realized through the market. The regulation of the market itself must demonstrate their economic efficacy through commercial calculation. The system of the transitional economy is unthinkable without the control of the ruble. This presupposes, in its turn, that the ruble is at par. Without a firm monetary unit, commercial accounting can only increase the chaos.[64]

Socialism, in the sense of the period of transition from capitalism to communism, is thus to be understood not so much in terms of any specific economic measures – for example, the nationalization of the means of production – but as the *political* framework, resting on soviet democracy, in which capitalist relations of production are progressively abolished. As the above passage indicates (and many others from both Trotsky and Lenin could have been cited), this transition period would be characterized in economic terms by various combinations of socialist planning and market mechanisms. Nevertheless, market and plan are not to be thought of as socially neutral techniques: they represent two different modes of production – respectively capitalism and communism – co-existing uneasily in a socialist political order.[65] The dictatorship of the proletariat is conceived in classical Marxism as a preliminary to communism: therefore the articulation of plan and market is one in which the former increasingly comes to prevail over the latter. Rather than a static 'market socialism', the transition period is characterized by the dynamic movement *away* from the market. To preserve the market as the basic regulator of economic life is to maintain conditions likely to generate inequalities that would become new bases of exploitation and liable to produce sharp fluctuations in output and unemployment and uncontrolled damage to the natural environment.

The idea of a marketless communist society is one of the main objects of Nove's derision. He argues that such a society presupposes the existence of abundance, defined as 'a sufficiency to meet requirements at zero price, leaving no reasonable person dissatisfied or seeking more of anything (or at least of anything reproducible)'. Such a condition would remove 'conflict over resource-allocation, since by definition there is enough for everyone, and so there are no mutually exclusive choices, no opportunity is foregone and therefore there is no opportunity-cost'. Nove dismisses this assumption as Utopian. Abundance is unattainable: in the first place, 'over half the world's population is very poor indeed', and 'the resources needed to bring them up to the levels already attained by, say, the skilled workers of Western Europe will surely not be available in the lifetime of our children's children'; secondly, 'absolute scarcity' will persist in the sense that some resources – 'land in the centre of cities, fish in the North Sea, perhaps oil' – either cannot be obtained in greater quantities or only at a rising cost; thirdly, 'relative scarcity' is endemic to the human condition, since needs grow, or, once satiated, are replaced by new ones: '[i]ndeed, without rising expectations, new aspirations, one would have a very dreary world.'[66]

The most obvious weakness in Nove's argument lies in his attempt to explain world poverty by the scarcity of resources. Fred Pearce cites a 1984 FAO report according to which,

> using current Western farming methods, the world could produce enough food for up to 33 billion people, seven times the present population. Using somewhat less sophisticated farming methods, 15 billion people could be fed and, even if the whole world relied on primitive farming methods, using no fertilisers or pesticides, traditional seeds and no soil conservation methods, the present world population could still be comfortably fed . . . Overall, Africa could, with primitive methods, feed 2.7 times its current population, says the FAO.[67]

Third World poverty, as we saw in section 4.1 above, is a consequence of prevailing social relations, not of scarcity. It is an indication of the apologetic drift of Nove's defence of the market that he suggests otherwise. His claims concerning the absolute scarcity of natural resources other than food are equally suspect. For example, Alexander Zucker of Oak Ridge National Laboratory in Tennessee estimates that it appears unlikely that the world will run short of any element before 2050. This provides considerable time to develop new technology to economically exploit lower grade and alternative ones to bring some thirty elements into essentially infinite supply and to use these elements in developing substitutes to satisfy the requirements of modern civilized societies.

Zucker calculates that the investment required by the year 2100 to achieve this objective would amount to $10 trillion, less than 0.2 per cent of cumulative world gross national product.[68]

The upshot of such estimates should not be to encourage complacency. One of the greatest challenges facing humankind is to make the investments necessary to support the world's population at an adequate level of living and to overcome any scarcities of essential resources without adding to, indeed while beginning to reverse, the destruction of the environment. It is hard to see how this task is to be performed without considerable planning at the global level. Yet the effect of Nove's arguments is to discourage the search for the political transformations and economic mechanisms required for such planning. Let us then consider his contention that the endurance of relative scarcities makes reliance on the market unavoidable.

This is, in fact, none other than a standard axiom of neo-classical economics, the insatiability of human wants. Wants are infinite: the satisfaction of a want at a certain level of intensity simply gives rise either to the demand for its more intense satisfaction or to its replacement by a new want. This process constantly recreates scarcity and therefore conflict. The market provides the most efficient and democratic mechanism for resolving these conflicts by measuring the intensity of people's wants for a particular item by the amount of money they are prepared to pay for it. The premiss of this argument – the insatiability of wants – cannot simply be dismissed by Marxists since they have an expansive conception of human nature. Marx writes, for example: 'Man is distinguished from all other animals by the limitless and flexible nature of his needs.'[69] The development of the productive forces involves the expansion of both human powers and human needs, even though many of the latter go unsatisfied, or are satisfied only to a limited degree, in class society. But needs are not the same as wants. Even ordinary usage tends to register the difference between the two concepts. It is possible to need x without being aware of it, but one is necessarily conscious of wanting x. This conceptual difference indicates the greater objectivity of needs, their source in a person's basic interests, rather than in her passing desires.

I may need to give up smoking, but not want to.[70]

This distinction between objective needs and subjective wants is implicit in Norman Geras's argument against the idea of communist abundance as 'abundance relative to a "limitless and flexible" notion of needs; in the sense, that is, of everyone being able to do whatever they might conceivably feel themselves as needing to':

> If by way of means of self-development you need a violin and I need a racing bicycle, this, one may assume, will be all right. But if I need an enormously large area, say Australia, to wander around in or generally use as I see fit undisturbed by the presence of other people, then this will obviously not be all right. No conceivable abundance could satisfy needs of self-development of this magnitude, given only a modest incidence of them across some population, and it is not difficult to think of needs that are much less excessive of which the same will be true.[71]

Geras concludes that communism involves 'abundance relative to some standard of "reasonable" needs which, large and generous as it may be possible for it to be, still falls short of any fantasy of abundance without limits'.[72] Now if we identify such 'reasonable' needs in the first instance with what are sometimes called 'basic needs' for such items as food, clothing, shelter, heating, light, education, and transport, then it becomes clear that with respect to these goods and services abundance in Nove's sense – supply at zero price – is attainable. Lange noted the tendency for the demand for certain commodities (he uses the example of salt) to become inelastic: 'If the price of such a commodity is below, and the consumer's income is above a certain minimum, the commodity is treated by the consumer *as if it were a free good*.' Where the demand for goods is thus saturated, 'free sharing can be used as a method of distribution'. The cost of producing such goods is shared collectively, but they are supplied free to individual consumers:

> Such a sector exists also in capitalist society, comprising, for example, free education, free medical services by social insurance, public parks, and all the collective wants in Cassel's sense (e.g. street lighting). It is quite conceivable that as wealth increases this sector increases, too, and an increasing number of commodities are distributed by free sharing until, finally, all the prime necessities of life are provided in this way, the distribution by the price system being confined to better qualities and luxuries. Thus Marx's second phase of communism may be gradually approached.[73]

There are, of course, numerous objections to this vision of an economy in which basic needs are met through the free provision of goods and services. Some are strictly economic and concern, for example, the difficulties apparently posed by the diverse ways in which even basic needs can be met – everyone needs clothing but who would want to live in a society where everyone dressed the same? – and by the changing boundaries between basic and non-basic needs caused by technical innovations and rising expectations (consider, for example, the significance accorded to consumer durables such as television sets and washing machines in modern industrial societies). It does not seem, however, that these represent insuperable difficulties for a communist society: resources could, for example, be set aside for groups of citizens wishing to explore innovations and mechanisms could be devised (including, perhaps, limited forms of market) to test the social demand for their products. It is also clear that much more thought needs to be given to the nature of democratic forms of planning involving horizontal connections between different production units and between producers and consumers rather than the vertical structure of control binding central planners, industrial ministries, and enterprises in the Stalinist command economy. But it is nothing but neo-liberal dogmatism to insist, as Nove and his co-thinkers do, that the *only* form these horizontal relationships can take is that of the market.[74] A second set of objections concern what are claimed to be the excessive requirements made of human nature in such a society. Surely the increases in productivity and output required to sustain even the 'reasonable' abundance defended by Geras can only be achieved by means of material incentives based on the rewards for individual effort reflected in the price obtained for the product of this effort on the market? And if this is so, then a marketless communist society is a contradiction in terms, since its material presuppositions depend on the existence of the market.

Marx does indeed accept the necessity of material incentives during the transition to communism, where income differences reflect individuals' productive contributions. But things go differently in communism itself, where the social product is distributed according to needs, not labour. Marx spells out the preconditions of this state of affairs in a famous passage in 'The Critique of the Gotha Programme':

> In a higher phase of communist society, after the enslaving subordination of the individual to the division of labour, and thereby also the antithesis between mental and physical labour has vanished; after

labour has become not only a means of life but life's prime want; after the productive forces have also increased with the all-round development of the individual, and all the springs of common wealth flow more abundantly — only then can the narrow horizon of bourgeois right be crossed in its entirety and society inscribe on its banners: From each according to his abilities, to each according to his needs![75]

Perhaps the crucial claim Marx makes here is that under communism labour will become 'life's prime want'. This reflects the belief, central to his theory of human nature, that labour is not merely the activity through which human beings meet their needs but also, potentially, the sphere in which they can most fully realize themselves. The contrast is brought out by this wonderful observation, buried in Marx's economic manuscripts: 'Milton produced *Paradise Lost* for the same reason that a silk worm produces silk. It was an activity of *his* nature. Later he sold the product for £5.'[76] Marx's prediction is that, once their basic needs are met, people will fulfil themselves through those forms of work which they discover are 'activities of their nature'. Marx does not believe, however, that 'labour [which] becomes attractive work, the individual's self-realization, . . . becomes mere fun, mere amusement, as Fourier, with *grisette*-like naïvety, conceives it. Really free working, e.g. composing, is at the same time precisely the most damned seriousness, the most intense exertion.'[77] His vision of communism is thus one in which human beings fulfil themselves through demanding but creative activity. How realistic a view is this?

One difficulty is posed by the likelihood of there being socially necessary activities which no-one finds fulfilling. Fourier assumed a pre-established harmony, written into the structure of nature itself, between the variety of social needs and the diversity of human passions: thus, small boys' love of dirt would solve the problem of who collects the refuse under communism (a belief which suggests that Fourier did not spend much time in the company of small children). Marx makes no such assumption. Indeed, in one famous passage he argues that '[t]he realm of freedom actually begins only where labour which is determined by necessity and mundane considerations ceases; thus in the very nature of things it lies beyond the sphere of actual material production', which 'remains a realm of necessity'. Consequently, 'that development of human energy which is an end in itself, the true end of freedom', depends on 'the shortening of the working day . . . as its basic prerequisite'.[78] Some labour thus remains, even under communism, a burden, performed only as 'a means of life', though now less for the individual than for society as a whole. But how will this burden, however reduced by increases in productivity making possible much shorter working hours, be distributed? This question is best addressed in the context of the problem of conflict in a communist society, which I consider below.

A common objection to Marx's account of work under communism is that he unrealistically expects the abolition of the division of labour. A particular object of derision is his celebrated prediction in *The German Ideology* that

> in communist society, where nobody has one exclusive sphere of activity but each can become accomplished in any branch he wishes, society regulates the general production and thus makes possible for me to hunt in the morning, fish in the afternoon, rear cattle in the evening, criticize after dinner, just as I have a mind, without ever becoming hunter, fisherman, shepherd or critic.[79]

One of the striking things about this passage is that the pursuits it lists are all pre-industrial. It is hard indeed to see how a less pastoral communism could do without all specialization: could I switch as easily from, say, brain surgery to aircraft design as from one of Marx's rural activities to another? Could I do it all? Ali Rattansi notes that in later writings such as *Capital* Marx tends to lay far more emphasis on the material constraints imposed by the 'realm of necessity' and to focus on abolishing the division between mental and manual labour as part of the process through which workers acquire collective control over production.[80] G. A. Cohen regards, however, even the later Marx as insufficiently realistic. The idea of 'the all-round development of the individual' is, according to Cohen, Utopian since it is in general impossible for individuals fully to develop all their capacities. In any case, self-fulfilment may often lie in specialized concentration on some particular ability or set of abilities: would Rembrandt have realized himself more fully (or society benefited more) if he had not been exclusively a painter?[81]

These criticisms do not, however, affect the central thrust of Marx's account of work under communism. His chief objection to the division of labour is that occupation is fate: one's particular position in this division is unchosen and yet determines one's life-chances. This is made clear in the lines immediately preceding the famous passage from *The German Ideology*:

> as soon as the division of labour comes into being, each man has a particular, exclusive sphere of activity which is forced upon him and

from which he cannot escape. He is a hunter, a fisherman, a shepherd, or a critical critic; and must remain so if he does not want to lose his means of livelihood.[82]

The problem thus identified is what Marx calls in the passage from 'The Critique of the Gotha Programme' cited earlier 'the enslaving subordination of the individual to the division of labour'. Abolishing *this* does not imply doing away with all specialization. It means rather that people should have access to the training required to perform the activities that they believe will fulfil them, and that they also are provided with real opportunities (retraining etc.) to change from one activity to another. The related abolition of 'the antithesis between mental and physical labour' requires further changes: for example, the transformation of an education system which prepares most people for subordinate, low-paid work, whether manual or white-collar, and the removal of the material privileges, social power, and cultural prestige attached to certain occupations some of which at least (for example, skilled medical personnel) would be required in a communist society.

Changes of this nature do not seem to be beyond the bounds of material feasibility. Indeed, various trends in contemporary society – for example, the increasing automation of material production and the associated diffusion of the skills involved in the use of computers – facilitate them. Marx's claim about work under communism is simply that, once these changes have been made, society will be able to meet its needs at the high, though not Utopian, standards of reasonable abundance primarily by encouraging people to fulfil themselves through creative activity. Is this so ridiculous a belief? Arguably one of the prime inequalities of modern capitalism is that fulfilment in work is largely the preserve of the ruling class itself and of the new middle class of professionals, managers and administrators occupying an intermediary position between wage-labour and capital.[83] The existence of an unsatisfied need for creative work is indicated by the vast range of 'leisure' activities pursued in the main by those in subordinate labouring positions. The wager of communism involves tapping this well of, at best, privatized creativity.

The transformations involved in the attainment of communism are, as we have seen, subject to the material constraints of the 'realm of necessity'. This implies both that people may have to spend some of their time performing unfulfilling work and that some of their wants will not be met. Both these facts are likely to give rise to conflict. Even in respect of those basic needs fully meeting which constitutes communist abundance conflicts may arise. There might, for one thing, be argument over which needs should be treated as basic for these purposes: food and clothing are pretty clearly basic needs but what about, say, having a television set? There might also be conflicts over the relative priority of different needs – of, for example, abolishing primary poverty in the Third World compared to improving the European housing stock. And needs can be met in different ways: is access to a washing machine best secured through individual ownership or collective provision? Some of these conflicts, one might argue, reflect problems that would arise in the process of constructing Marx's 'higher phase of communist society' rather than difficulties inherent in communism itself. But even if we grant this, it is not true of all of them, and, given that Marx conceives of communism as a dynamic state of affairs, powered by the pursuit of fulfilment in creative work, technical innovations and rising expectations would be likely to produce new occasions of conflict.

For many, this recognition that Marx's communism is not Fourier's Harmony, that the abolition of classes is not equivalent to the eradication of conflict, amounts to an admission of defeat. We have seen, for example, that David Held ascribes to Marx the view that '[t]he end of class means the end of any legitimate basis for disputes' (section 4.2 above). Jon Elster similarly accuses Marx of believing that 'social decision-making can occur without conflict, by unanimous approval or election'.[84] Now, not only is there no evidence that Marx believed anything so silly, but such evidence as does exist points in the opposite direction. In the first place, communism is a society governed by the goal of individual self-realization. It is, he says in the *Manifesto*, 'an association in which the free development of each is the condition of the free development of all'.[85] Elsewhere he calls freedom man's 'positive power to assert his true individuality'.[86] This view of communism as liberating individual capacities surely implies a society characterized by diversity – unless, like Elster, one attributes to Marx 'the idea that all individuals have the same inborn capacities – both quantitatively and qualitatively'.[87] But not only is this idea quite contrary to the tenor of Marx's discussions of communism (why stress individuality if individuals are all the same?), but it is explicitly rejected by him. One of the problems he identifies with the contribution principle operative during the transition to communism, which rewards people according to the labour they perform, is that 'one man is superior to another physically or mentally' and so contributes and is rewarded more. The contribution principle applies an 'equal standard' to 'unequal individuals (and they would not be different individuals if they were not unequal)'. The superiority of the needs principle ('From each according to his abilities, to each according to his needs') is precisely that it attends to the differences in individual capacities and requirements.[88]

Far from imposing uniformity, a communist society would involve a proliferation of diversity. Perry Anderson argues that

> a socialist society would be a far more complicated one than what we have today. It seems perfectly clear that if you actually had a socialist society in which production, power, and culture were genuinely democratized, you would have an enormous multiplication of different ways of living. People would choose how to live, and it is perfectly obvious that people have different temperaments, gifts, and values. These differences are suppressed and compressed within very narrow limits by the capitalist market and the inequalities of bourgeois society.[89]

This 'multiplication of different ways of living' would inevitably give rise to conflict. Given that communism presupposes reasonable rather than unlimited abundance, not all goals can be realized, and everyone may have to compromise their goals to some extent in order to take part in the 'labour which is determined by necessity and mundane considerations' and without which even reasonable abundance will not be reproduced. Diversity thus, under any realistic conditions, implies conflict. Marx concedes as much when he writes: 'The bourgeois mode of production is the last antagonistic form of the social process of production – antagonistic not in the sense of individual antagonism but of an antagonism that emanates from the individuals' social conditions of existence.' Nor is this merely the grudging acceptance of an unwelcome reality: in the following sentence he says that the overthrow of capitalism marks the end of the 'prehistory of human society', a remark which indicates how far Marx was from the idea, popularized by Fukuyama, of an 'end of history'.[90] As humankind enters the period of its real history, 'individual antagonism' might be expected to become one of the main driving forces of social change in a world no longer dominated by the contradiction between the forces and relations of production.

Trotsky offers a more concrete account of the way in which conflict would provide communist society with its dynamism:

> There would be the struggle for one's opinion, for one's project, for one's taste. In the measure in which political struggles will be eliminated – and in a society where there will be no classes, there will be no such struggles – the liberated passions will be channelized into

technique, into construction which also includes art ... All forms of life, such as the cultivation of land, the planning of human habitations, the building of theatres, the methods of socially educating children, the solution of scientific problems, the creation of new styles, will engross all and everybody. People will divide into 'parties' over the question of a new gigantic canal, or the distribution of oases in the Sahara (such a question will exist too), over the regulation of the weather and the climate, over a new theatre, over chemical hypotheses, over two competing tendencies in music, and over a best system of sports.[91]

It is thus no part of classical Marxism to equate communism with the absence of conflict. Two questions then arise. First, how does 'individual antagonism' differ from the conflicts of class society? The answer is surely that the kind of disputes that arise in communist society will not involve systematic differences in social power reflecting individuals' control or lack of control over the productive forces. Conflicts are likely to arise because individuals differ, in Anderson's phrase, in 'temperaments, gifts, and values'. But these differences are not likely to lead to systematic social polarization such that the same sets of individuals line up against each other on every issue. I may agree with you that the motor car should be phased out of use but reject your proposal that the great metropolis be run down in favour of smaller, dispersed settlements. Such differences exist today, but individuals' dependence on their position in antagonistic relations of production (i.e. their class position) to realize their goals, however diverse, means that global polarizations of interest develop. A communist society, by equalizing individuals' position in the relations of production, would make possible the kind of pluralist order which Anglo-Saxon political scientists claim to be a feature of Western liberal democracies, but which is negated by the underlying inequalities in the distribution of productive resources under capitalism. Each issue would produce its own division of opinion, so that individuals would line up differently on various issues, producing a kaleidoscope of overlapping and ephemeral 'parties', emerging in response to, and canvassing support around some specific question, and dissolving or declining as it was at least temporarily resolved.[92]

Secondly, how exactly *would* such conflicts be resolved? The answer is again evident enough: through some procedure for making decisions based on the principle of majority rule. Lenin explicitly rejects the idea that the withering away of the state under communism is equivalent to 'the advent of a system of society in which the principle of subordination of the minority to the majority will not be observed'.[93] Marx draws a similar distinction when he predicts that under communism 'the public power will lose its political character. Political power, properly so called, is merely the organized power of one class for oppressing another.'[94] Classical Marxism thus distinguishes between the state, which is a phenomenon of class society, and the 'public power' which exists even under communism, where it is governed by the majority principle. The rationale for this contrast is provided by Marx's and Lenin's conception of the state as a specialized apparatus of coercion which both is a consequence of, and serves to perpetuate the existence of class antagonisms. Hence the significance of the emergence of forms of workers' power, beginning with the Commune, which, as Engels had put it, 'ceased to be a state in the true sense of the term'.[95] Socialist democracy, a form of state involving, as we have seen, the systematic participation of the labouring majority in self-government, points towards a society in which no specialized apparatus of coercion is any longer necessary. This society is communism, Lenin says, 'for there is *nobody* to be suppressed – "nobody" in the sense of a *class*, of a systematic struggle against a definite section of the population'.[96] It does not follow that such a society can do without a 'public power', in other words, mechanisms for resolving conflicts, and taking and enforcing decisions that are based on the democratic procedures developed during the long struggles for emancipation first within feudal and then capitalist societies.

Many will not be satisfied by this distinction between the state in class society and the 'public power' under communism. They may want reassurance that there would not be other enduring, systematic, social polarizations than that of class – nationality or gender, for example.[97] Or they may demand some more detailed account of decision-making mechanisms under communism and of their evolution out of soviet institutional forms. These are legitimate questions. Nevertheless, communism as conceived by classical Marxism is not vulnerable to the objection raised by Held that it lacks 'a place for systematically encouraging and tolerating disagreement and debate on public matters' (section 4.2 above). On the contrary, everything written on the subject by Marx, Lenin, and Trotsky suggests that communist society would be characterized by a dynamic and diverse public life. What, then, is the sense of claiming, as Trotsky does in the passage cited above, that 'political struggles will be eliminated' under communism? It is only when politics is understood as the process through which classes with antagonistic interests struggle to obtain, retain or influence state power that we can talk of an 'end of politics' under communism.[98] There are several connected reasons for insisting on such a restrictive usage of the term 'politics'. For one thing, conflicts are likely to be of a far less intense character when people's basic needs are met. Any half-serious survey of contemporary world politics will register a direct relationship between the extent and bitterness of power struggles and the degree of material deprivation in the society in question. Secondly, conflicts under communism are likely, as we have seen, to involve different groupings of individuals according to the issue under discussion. What is supposedly one of the virtues of liberal democracy can actually be realized – since anyone in a minority on one issue is likely to be compensated by being in the majority on others. These properties of conflicts under communism – their lack of intensity and promotion of diverse groupings – imply, thirdly, that in normal circumstances the acceptance of social decisions is unlikely to require much coercion to enforce them. In all these respects public life under communism would be fundamentally different from politics in even the most liberal of capitalist democracies. To give both activities the same name could only be apologetic in its effect, since it would serve to conceal the difference in kind between societies characterized by class exploitation and organized state violence, and communism, whose existence depends on the absence of these features.

The foregoing discussion of what one might call 'feasible communism' has drawn heavily on the texts of classical Marxism. This is in part as a response to what Geras has recently called the 'obloquy' and 'travesty' which this tradition has suffered at the hands of contemporary writers of the left.[99] The account of communism sketched out by Marx and his successors is simply not vulnerable to most of the criticisms levelled against it. It does not follow that this account is a complete and satisfactory one, although it is not clear how far it can be further developed without future experiments in socialist democracy. For all its faults, however, the Marxian vision of communism has one vast strength. Marx famously criticized the Utopian socialists, both because of their erroneous theories of social change, which usually relied on the liberating work of an enlightened elite, and because they sought to anticipate the results of a long-drawn-out historical process of transformation by offering detailed descriptions of the future society. But there is a sense – a good sense – in which Marx is as Utopian as Fourier: both refuse to treat existing society as the benchmark of human possibility. Nothing is more striking about the contemporary Western left than its utterly impoverished vision of social change. The success of Nove's *Economics of Feasible Socialism* reflects an acceptance by repentant Stalinists and chastened social-democrats alike of 'really existing capitalism' as defining the horizons of possible change: all that we can hope for is Adam Michnik's 'market with a human face'. The implications of this capitulation are staggering. Socialism, we are led to believe, must adapt itself to a market from whose delights most of the world are excluded. It must accept as a success story societies whose great cities – New York and London for example – now set abject beggary and profligate wealth cheek by jowl more blatantly than at any time this century. It must acknowledge as the most effective social bond the instrumental relationship of exchange between the buyers and sellers of commodities. It must ask the producers of wealth to acquiesce in the same position of subordination and exploitation to which they have been condemned throughout the history of capitalism. It must confine itself meekly to regulating and moderating the effects of a system whose global reach and anarchic fluctuations have mightily grown in the past quarter century. Is this really the best that humankind can do? Can a species with an astonishing history of technical and social innovations packed into a few millennia really accept the market as the *nec plus ultra* of its development? Marx distinguished between the 'limited bourgeois form' in which the productive forces grow under capitalism and '[t]he absolute working-out of [humankind's] creative potentialities, with no presupposition other than the previous historic development, which makes this totality of development, i.e. the development of all human powers as such, as the end in itself'.[100] From this latter perspective, of the development of human productive powers across a succession of limited social forms, it is not the believer in the market as a final resting point, but Marx, who is the realist.

CONCLUSION

In one respect the East European revolutions have simplified matters enormously. There can now be no doubt that we live in a single, unified world system. The illusion that there was a 'socialist third of the world', that a separate, post-capitalist socio-economic system was in the process of construction, has been destroyed, along with most of the regimes supposedly embodying that system. The impact of that colossal piece of tidying up has been felt well beyond Europe: substantial parts of Africa and the Arab East, where the Stalinist one-party state provided a political model for regimes often paying only the most casual lip-service to socialist ideals, experienced large-scale popular protests at the turn of the 1980s. But the implications of the collapse of Stalinism go much further. The East European revolutions have accelerated a process already under way – the unification of world politics. Various factors have promoted this tendency: the globalization of capital, the industrialization of portions of the Third World, vast movements of people from the poor to the rich countries, the development of transcontinental telecommunications networks which mean that billions can watch *Dallas*, or the opening of the Berlin Wall, or Nelson Mandela's release. The effect is to encourage people to draw analogies between their situations and those of others, and to take inspiration from apparently remote struggles. Azeris in the USSR reacted to the breaking open of the Berlin Wall by tearing down the border fences separating them from their fellow Turks in Iran. Anti-poll-tax demonstrators in Whitehall ran down the Union Jack and ripped out its centre, following the example of Romanians during the Christmas Revolution. Of course, there are powerful counter-trends – above all, the renewed strength of national and religious identities partly in reaction to the bewildering and threatening dynamism of a world system that respects no state boundaries. Nevertheless, a pronounced tendency to form judgements and take action in the light of a sense of global developments undoubtedly exists.

More than that, however: in São Paulo and Warsaw, Johannesburg and London, Seoul and Moscow, Cairo and New York, the same basic choices are posed. Do we let the market rip, with all the disastrous consequences that will have for the well-being of humankind and perhaps the survival of the earth? Do we seek to humanize it, as social democracy has sought ineffectually to do since the beginning of the century? Or do we struggle to replace the anarchy and injustice of capitalism with a social system based on the collective and democratic control of the world's resources by working people? It should be clear enough that I prefer the third of these alternatives and that I believe that the classical Marxist tradition represents the best way of pursuing it. 'Best' does not mean perfect: there are no doubt many questions which revolutionary socialists have yet to address or to answer satisfactorily. Nevertheless, classical Marxism is the *only* tradition with the theoretical and political resources needed to confront the issues currently facing us. As I have tried to show, it is radically at odds with its monstrous Stalinist distortion. Secondly, it can provide a historical materialist analysis of both the rise and the fall of this distortion. Thirdly, Marx and his successors developed a perfectly feasible strategy for overthrowing capitalism and constructing a better society in its place.

The East European revolutions thus represent a moment of both danger and hope for socialists: danger because the collapse of Stalinism is all too readily interpreted, not simply by the defenders but also by many erstwhile opponents of capitalism, as the death of any kind of socialist alternative to the status quo; hope because the Marxist tradition can finally rid itself of the muck of (no longer) 'really existing socialism'. There are good reasons for believing that, once the immediate clamour celebrating the 'triumph of the West' dies down, the need for visions of an alternative society to capitalism and for strategies to realize them will reassert itself. In a justly famous passage of the *Manifesto*, Marx praises capitalism for its dynamism:

> Constant revolutionizing of production, uninterrupted disturbance of all social conditions, everlasting uncertainty and agitation distinguish the bourgeois epoch from all earlier ones. All fixed, fast-frozen relations, with their train of ancient and venerable prejudices and opinions, are swept away, all new-formed ones become antiquated before they can ossify. All that is solid melts into air, all that is holy is profaned, and man is at last compelled to face with sober senses, his real conditions of life, and his relations with his kind.[1]

The East European revolutions have swept away one set of 'fixed, fast-frozen relations', to the immediate benefit of multinational capitalism. But the experience of integration into the world market is likely to place the illusions in liberal capitalism which were one factor in these upheavals, and which still play their part in the unfolding crisis in the USSR, under increasing pressure. Many in what we now can no longer call the Eastern bloc will find themselves 'at last compelled to face with sober senses, [their] real conditions of life'. What conclusions they draw will depend on the political alternatives available: the growth of xenophobic nationalism and racism in Eastern and Western Europe alike gives some indication of the kind of politics which people's awakening from their dreams of the market may nurture. It is essential that the Marxist tradition should be available among these alternatives, to offer an internationalism which is not that of multinational corporations and stock exchanges but which reflects the global lines of conflict between capital and labour, and to defend a reason which expresses not the pursuit of individual self-interest but of humankind's ability collectively to direct their own lives and to regulate their relationship with nature. Since the 1920s that tradition has been confined to the margins of political life, persecuted, derided, and (perhaps worst of all) reduced to an academic specialism. Now classical Marxism can finally shake itself free of the Stalinist incubus and seize the opportunities offered by a world experiencing greater 'uncertainty and agitation' than for many decades. It is time to resume unfinished business.

NOTES

Key to Abbreviations

FT   *Financial Times*
IS   *International Socialism*
LCW   V. I. Lenin, *Collected Works* (45 vols, Moscow, 1974)
MECW K. Marx and F. Engels, *Collected Works* (50 vols published or in preparation, London, 1975–)
NLR   *New Left Review*

CHAPTER 1   The End of Socialism?

1. Quoted in E. J. Hobsbawm, *Echoes of the Marseillaise* (London, 1990), pp. ix–x.
2. R. Rorty, *Contingency, Irony, and Solidarity* (Cambridge, 1989), p. 94.
3. For an account and analysis of the democracy movement, see C. Hore, 'China: Tiananmen Square and After', *IS*, 2:44 (1989).
4. The transformation of Eastern Europe is captured by Tim Garton Ash in a brilliant set of snapshots, *We the People* (Cambridge, 1990), and analysed by Chris Harman in 'The Storm Breaks', *IS*, 2:46 (1990).
5. H. R. Trevor-Roper, 'The Crowning Revolution', *The Independent Magazine*, 6 Jan. 1990.
6. 'The State of Europe: Christmas Eve 1989', *Granta*, 30 (1990), p. 131.
7. F. Fukuyama, 'The End of History?', *The National Interest*, Summer 1989, pp. 3, 4, 9, 18.
8. P. Q. Hirst, 'Endism', *London Review of Books*, 23 Nov. 1989, p. 14. Other critiques of Fukuyama include J. Rees, 'Goodbye to All That?', *Socialist Worker Review*, Sep. 1989; J. Steele, E. Mortimer, and G. Stedman Jones, 'The End of History?', *Marxism Today*, Nov. 1989; and J. McCarney, 'History under the Hammer', *Times Higher Education Supplement*, 1 Dec. 1989.
9. Mortimer, 'End', p. 29.

10. Fukuyama, 'End', p. 18.
11. *Independent*, 5 Feb. 1990.
12. P. Johnson, 'Demise of Crooked Creed', *Spectator*, 17 Feb. 1990, p. 21.
13. J. Rees, 'Infuriating Mixture', *Socialist Worker Review*, Nov. 1989, p. 32.
14. T. G. Ash, 'Ten Days that Stirred the World', *Spectator*, 2 Dec. 1989, p. 9.
15. S. Rushdie, 'Is Nothing Sacred?', *Granta*, 31 (1990), p. 109.
16. R. L. Heilbroner, *Beyond Boom and Crash* (London, 1979), p. 79.
17. Quoted in J. Slovo, *Has Socialism Failed?* (London, 1990), p. 7.
18. E. J. Hobsbawm, 'Waking from History's Great Dream', *Independent on Sunday* Sunday Review, 4 Feb. 1990, pp. 3–5.
19. C. Myant, 'Living with Lenin', *7 Days*, 24 Feb. 1990.
20. M. Jacques, 'After Communism', *Marxism Today*, Jan. 1990, p. 37.
21. F. Halliday, 'The Ends of the Cold War', *NLR*, 180 (1990), pp. 12, 18, 35. Halliday develops a 'Deutscherite' analysis of East–West conflict in *The Making of the Second Cold War* (London, 1983).
22. *Independent*, 22 Feb. 1990.
23. M. Lewin, *The Making of the Soviet System* (London, 1985), p. 191.
24. Id., *Lenin's Last Struggle* (London, 1973). The main issue in the dying Lenin's dispute with Stalin was the 'Great Russian chauvinism' displayed by the latter as Commissar of Nationalities. Even Richard Pipes in his bitterly anti-Bolshevik study, *The Formation of the Soviet Union*, rev. edn (Cambridge, Mass., 1964), cannot conceal the gulf separating Lenin's insistence that 'the fundamental interest of proletarian solidarity ... demand[s] that in this case we should never treat the national question formally but always take into account the difference in the relationship of the oppressed or small nation toward the oppressing or large nation' (quoted, p. 285) and the institutionalization of Russian dominance in the USSR from its foundation in 1924.
25. 'Bukharin–Kamenev Meeting', Appendix A, in L. D. Trotsky, *The Challenge of the Left Opposition (1928–9)* (New York, 1981), pp. 379–83.
26. See the accounts in A. I. Solzhenitsyn, *The Gulag Archipelago*, II (London, 1976), pp. 303–7, 372–6, and 'M.B.', 'The Trotskyists in Vorkuta Prison Camp', in T. Ali (ed.), *The Stalinist Legacy* (Harmondsworth, 1984).
27. Notable examples of the recent theoretical development of historical materialism include L. Althusser and E. Balibar, *Reading Capital* (London, 1970), B. Hindess and P. Q. Hirst, *Pre-Capitalist Modes of Production* (London, 1975), E. P. Thompson, *The Poverty of Theory and Other Essays* (London, 1978), G. A. Cohen, *Karl Marx's Theory of History* (Oxford, 1978), P. Anderson, *Arguments within English Marxism* (London, 1980), G. E. M. de Ste Croix, *The Class Struggle in the Ancient Greek World* (London, 1981), T. H. Aston and C. H. E. Philpin, *The Brenner Debate* (Cambridge, 1985), C. Harman, 'Base

and Superstructure', *IS*, 2:32 (1986), and A. Callinicos, *Making History* (Cambridge, 1987).

28. E. Gellner, *State and Society in Soviet Thought* (Oxford, 1988), p. 163.
29. See esp. A. Giddens, *A Contemporary Critique of Historical Materialism* (London, 1981), M. Mann, *The Sources of Social Power*, I (Cambridge, 1986), R. Unger, *Politics* (3 vols, Cambridge, 1987), E. Gellner, *Plough, Sword and Book* (Oxford, 1988), and W. G. Runciman, *A Treatise on Social Theory*, II (Cambridge, 1989). Perry Anderson surveys what he calls 'the appearance of a series of large-scale theories of history, comparable in scope to that adumbrated by Marx, and conceived to outmatch it' in Britain during the 1980s (Giddens, Mann, Runciman, Gellner) in 'A Culture in Contraflow – I', *NLR*, 180 (1990), pp. 51–73.
30. *MECW*, XXIV, p. 269.
31. Ibid., VI, p. 495.
32. H. Draper, 'The Two Souls of Socialism', *New Politics*, V:I (1966), *passim*. Draper elaborates his conception of Marxism in *Karl Marx's Theory of Revolution* (3 vols, New York, 1977, 1978, 1986).
33. See D. Hallas, *Trotsky's Marxism* (London, 1979), and A. Callinicos, *Trotskyism* (Milton Keynes, 1990), chs. 1–3.
34. T. Cliff, 'The Nature of Stalinist Russia', *Revolutionary Communist Party Internal Bulletin*, June 1948, p. 142; *State Capitalism in Russia* (London, 1988), p. 276.
35. C. Harman, 'Prospects for the Seventies: the Stalinist States', *IS*, 42 (1970), p. 19.

CHAPTER 2 The *Ancien Régime* and the Revolution

1. R. Pipes, *Russia under the Old Regime* (Harmondsworth, 1977).
2. S. Fitzpatrick, *The Russian Revolution 1917–1932* (Oxford, 1982), p. 3.
3. See P. Broué, *Révolution en Allemagne 1918–1923* (Paris, 1973), and C. Harman, *The Lost Revolution* (London, 1982).
4. C. Rosenberg, *1919* (London, 1987), and P. Spriano, *The Occupation of the Factories* (London, 1975).
5. N. I. Bukharin, *Imperialism and World Economy* (London, 1972).
6. L. D. Trotsky, *1905* (Harmondsworth, 1973), chs 1–4; see also id., *The History of the Russian Revolution* (3 vols, London, 1967), I, ch. 1. A remarkably similar perspective on the Russian Revolution to Trotsky's and Bukharin's is provided by the Tory historian Norman Stone in *The Eastern Front* (London, 1975), esp. chs 7, 8, 9, and 13. He concludes (p. 301): 'The Bolshevik Revolution was a fact before it happened'.
7. T. Cliff, *Lenin* (4 vols, London, 1975–9), and M. Liebman, *Leninism under Lenin* (London, 1975).

8. N. N. Sukhanov, *The Russian Revolution 1917* (Princeton, 1984), pp. 648–9.

9. A. Rabinowitch, *The Bolsheviks Come to Power* (London, 1979), pp. xx–xxi.

10. *The Bolsheviks and the October Revolution: Central Committee Minutes of the Russian Social-Democratic Labour Party (Bolsheviks) August 1917–February 1918* (London, 1974).

11. M. Ferro, *October 1917* (London, 1980), pp. 272, 274. See also, *inter alia*, Cliff, *Lenin*, II, S. Smith, *Red Petrograd* (Cambridge, 1983), D. Mandel, *The Petrograd Workers and the Fall of the Old Regime* (London, 1983), id., *The Petrograd Workers and the Soviet Seizure of Power* (London, 1984), and A. Rabinowitch, *Prelude to Revolution* (Bloomington, Indiana, 1968).

12. M. Lewin, *The Making of the Soviet System* (London, 1985), p. 199.

13. Quoted in P. Sedgewick, Introduction to V. Serge, *Memoirs of a Revolutionary 1901–1941* (Oxford, 1967), pp. xv–xvi.

14. Quoted in Ferro, *October 1917*, p. 148.

15. Cliff, *Lenin*, III, p. 113.

16. Mandel, *Petrograd Workers and Soviet Seizure*, p. 383.

17. Cliff, *Lenin*, III, chs 7–13.

18. *MECW*, V, p. 49.

19. *LCW*, XXVI, pp. 470–1; XXVII, p. 98.

20. Cliff, *Lenin*, IV, and D. Hallas, *The Comintern* (London, 1985).

21. *LCW*, XXX, p. 263.

22. A. Nove, *An Economic History of the USSR* (Harmondsworth, 1972), pp. 105–9. For a critical discussion of the concept of kulak in particular, see Lewin, *Making*, ch. 5.

23. See, for example, R. Medvedev, *The October Revolution* (London, 1979), Part Four.

24. *LCW*, XXXII, p. 48.

25. Ibid., p. 225.

26. See, for example, the summary of these debates in Nove, *Economic History*, ch. 5, and, in more detail, E. H. Carr, *Socialism in One Country 1924–1926*, II (London, 1959), Part III.

27. R. V. Daniels, 'Soviet Politics since Krushchev', in J. W. Strong (ed.), *The Soviet Union under Brezhnev and Kosygin* (New York, 1971), p. 20.

28. Fitzpatrick, *Russian Revolution*, ch. 5.

29. T. Cliff, *State Capitalism in Russia* (London, 1988), pp. 164–6.

30. See esp. M. Reiman, *The Birth of Stalinism* (London, 1987).

31. See, for example, Nove, *Economic History*, ch. 7, and Lewin, *Making*, Part II.

32. Nove, *Economic History*, pp. 142–8, 187–9.

33. J. V. Stalin, *Collected Works* (13 vols, Moscow, 1954–5), XIII, pp. 40–1.

34. *LCW*, XXIX, p. 153.

35. W. H. McNeill, *The Pursuit of Power* (Oxford, 1982), chs 7–9.
36. Nove, *Economic History*, p. 220.
37. See M. Ellman, 'Did the Agricultural Surplus Provide the Resources for the Increase in Investment in the USSR during the First Five-Year Plan?', *Economic Journal*, 85 (1975), and J. R. Miller and A. Nove, 'A Debate on Collectivization', *Problems of Communism*, Jul.–Aug. 1976.
38. D. Filtzer, *Soviet Workers and Stalinist Industrialization* (London, 1986), p. 91.
39. Lewin, *Making*, ch. 9.
40. Ellman, 'Agricultural Surplus', pp. 856–7.
41. Filtzer, *Soviet Workers, passim.* Compare T. W. Mason, 'The Workers' Opposition in Nazi Germany', *History Workshop*, 11 (1981).
42. M. Lewin, 'Society, State, and Ideology during the First Five-Year Plan', reprinted in Lewin, *Making*, p. 221.
43. G. Wheatcroft, 'On Assessing the Size of Forced Concentration Camp Labour in the Soviet Union, 1929–56', *Soviet Studies*, XXXIII:2 (1981), p. 286.
44. J. F. Hough and M. Fainsod, *How the Soviet Union is Governed* (Cambridge, Mass., 1979), pp. 176–7. Recent Western estimates such as this one tend to give much lower figures for the number of Stalin's victims than those which became popular in the USSR under Gorbachev.
45. Filtzer, *Soviet Workers*, pp. 131ff.
46. S. Fitzpatrick (ed.), *Cultural Revolution in Russia, 1928–31* (Bloomington, Indiana, 1978).
47. For example, Fitzpatrick, *Russian Revolution*, pp. 129ff.
48. See esp. Filtzer, *Soviet Workers*, pp. 48–9.
49. N. S. Timasheff, *The Great Retreat* (New York, 1946).
50. Cliff, *State Capitalism*, pp. 77–93.
51. Lewin, *Making*, pp. 236–7.
52. J. A. Getty, *Origins of the Great Purges* (Cambridge, 1985). But see Robert Conquest's very critical review, 'Purge and Revision', *Times Literary Supplement*, 9 May 1986.
53. S. Fitzpatrick, 'Cultural Revolution as Class War', in id. (ed.), *Cultural Revolution*, p. 39.
54. J. F. Hough, *Russia and the West*, 2nd edn (New York, 1990), pp. 18–22.
55. M. Lewin, *Political Undercurrents in Soviet Economic Debates* (London, 1975), p. 253.
56. See, for example, A. Nove, *The Soviet Economic System*, 3rd edn (London, 1986).
57. See R. Rosdolsky, *The Making of Marx's Capital* (London, 1977), and A. Callinicos, *Is there a Future for Marxism?* (London, 1982), chs 5 and 6.
58. Filtzer, *Soviet Workers*, p. 135. Filtzer denies that labour-power is a commodity in the USSR (pp. 259–60) but himself points to the

similarities of working-class behaviour in the USSR and in other repressive labour-shortage economies such as Nazi Germany (pp. 152–6).

59. Nove, *Soviet Economic System*, p. 203. For the 1930s, see, for example, Filtzer, *Soviet Workers*, pp. 52–3, and, for a theoretical discussion of the issues involved, see A. Callinicos, 'Wage-Labour and State Capitalism', *IS*, 2:12 (1981).

60. Cliff, *State Capitalism*, p. 47.

61. Ibid., p. 165.

62. Quoted in C. Harman, 'The Myth of Market Socialism', *IS*, 2:42 (1989), p. 49.

63. C. Harman, *Explaining the Crisis* (London, 1984), ch. 2.

64. E. Mandel, *The Second Slump* (London, 1980), pp. 147–8. For a critical appraisal of Mandel's more recent writing on the USSR, see C. Harman, 'From Trotsky to State Capitalism', *IS*, 2:47 (1990).

65. Quoted in C. Harman and A. Zebrowski, 'Glasnost – Before the Storm', *IS*, 2:39 (1988), p. 5.

66. M. Shachtman, *The Bureaucratic Revolution* (New York, 1962). See, for an assessment of Shachtman's analysis of Stalinism, T. Cliff, 'The Theory of Bureaucratic Collectivism: A Critique', Appendix 2 to Cliff, *State Capitalism*. It says much for the state of what passes for scholarship on the contemporary academic left that one leading American 'post-Marxist' should ascribe to Shachtman 'the famous thesis that Russia, by the mid 1930s had become a state capitalist regime': see S. Aronowitz, *The Crisis in Historical Materialism*, 2nd edn (London, 1990), p. 319. I discuss the tradition associated with Shachtman in *Trotskyism* (Milton Keynes, 1990), ch. 4.

67. F. Fehér and A. Heller, *Eastern Left, Western Left* (Cambridge, 1987), pp. 56, 59, 185.

68. *FT*, 21 Feb. 1990.

69. M. Haynes, 'Understanding the Soviet Crisis', *IS*, 2:34 (1987), pp. 6–20.

70. M. C. Kaser, editor's introduction to *An Economic History of Eastern Europe 1919–75*, I (Oxford, 1985), p. 9.

71. Hough, *Russia*, p. 237.

72. CIA estimates cited in C. Harman, 'The Storm Breaks', *IS*, 2:46 (1990), p. 31.

73. See, for example, the diagnoses discussed in Lewin, *Political Undercurrents*.

74. J. Kornai, *Growth, Shortage and Efficiency* (Oxford, 1982), p. 90.

75. M. Wolf, 'Death Rattle of the Stalinist War Economy', Survey on the Soviet Union, *FT*, 12 Mar. 1990.

76. Id., 'Measures of the Task Ahead', Survey on the Soviet Union, *FT*, 12 Mar. 1990.

77. These changes form the main theme of two books by Nigel Harris, *Of*

Bread and Guns (Harmondsworth, 1983), and *The End of the Third World* (London, 1986); for an attempt to qualify some of the more extreme claims made in them, see A. Callinicos, 'Imperialism, Capitalism and the State Today', *IS*, 2:35 (1987).

78. Quoted in Harris, *End*, p. 212 n. 9.
79. See C. Harman, *Class Struggles in Eastern Europe, 1945–83* (London, 1983), ch. 9.
80. See id., 'The Storm Breaks', pp. 44–7. The entire preceding analysis is heavily indebted to this article.
81. B. Kagarlitsky, *The Dialectic of Change* (London, 1990), p. 284.
82. M. Lewin, *The Gorbachev Phenomenon* (London, 1988), pp. 31–2.
83. Hough, *Russia*, p. 93.
84. See, for example, Kagarlitsky, *Dialectic*, ch. 6, and Lewin, *Gorbachev Phenomenon*, ch. 3.
85. Kagarlitsky, *Dialectic*, p. 292.
86. See K. M. Simis, *USSR – Secrets of a Corrupt Society* (London, 1982).
87. S. F. Cohen, 'The Friends and Foes of Change', in id. et al. (eds), *The Soviet Union since Stalin* (London, 1980).
88. Compare the very different accounts in Hough, *Russia*, chs 6–7, and Z. Medvedev, *Gorbachev*, rev. edn (Oxford, 1987), Part 1.
89. T. Ali, *Revolution from Above* (London, 1988), p. xii.
90. Medvedev, *Gorbachev*, pp. 191, 285.
91. A. de Tocqueville, *The Ancien Régime and the French Revolution* (London, 1966), p. 196.
92. C. Harman, 'The Stalinist States', *IS*, 42 (1970), p. 14.
93. T. G. Ash, *The Uses of Adversity* (Cambridge, 1989), p. 276.
94. P. Anderson, 'Modernity and Revolution', in C. Nelson and L. Grossberg (eds), *Marxism and the Interpretation of Culture* (Basingstoke, 1988), p. 332.
95. 'Themes', *NLR*, 178 (1989), pp. 1–2.
96. T. G. Ash, 'New Faces for Old in Eastern Europe', *Spectator*, 17 Mar. 1990, p. 9.
97. V. Havel, 'Anti-Political Politics', in J. Keane (ed.), *Civil Society and the State* (London, 1988), pp. 395, 392, 394.
98. N. Ascherson, 'Who Would Have Thought It?', *London Review of Books*, 8 Mar. 1990, p. 6. See also T. G. Ash, 'Does Central Europe Exist?', in id., *Uses*.
99. *FT*, 29 Nov. 1989.
100. N. Ascherson, 'Old Conflicts in the New Europe', *Independent on Sunday* Sunday Review, 18 Feb. 1990, p. 4.
101. L. D. Trotsky, *Writings (1933–34)* (New York, 1972), pp. 102–3.
102. Cliff, *State Capitalism*, p. 195.
103. T. G. Ash, *We the People* (Cambridge, 1990), p. 141.
104. J. Kuroń and K. Modzelewski, *A Revolutionary Socialist Manifesto* (London, 1968).

105. M. Matthews, *Privilege in the Soviet Union* (London, 1978).
106. See, for example, J. F. Hough, *The Soviet Prefects* (Cambridge, Mass., 1969).
107. *FT*, 3 Oct. 1989.
108. Ibid., 19 Jan. 1990.
109. Ibid., 13 Jan. 1990.
110. Ibid., 28 Feb. and 13 Mar. 1990.
111. Harman, 'The Storm Breaks', pp. 64ff.
112. *FT*, 13 Mar. 1990.
113. Ibid., 3 Oct. 1989.
114. L. D. Trotsky, *The Revolution Betrayed* (New York, 1972), p. 288.
115. *FT*, 17 Apr. 1990.
116. Ibid., 18 Apr. 1990.
117. Ash, *We the People*, p. 45.
118. *FT*, 21 May 1990.
119. Survey on the Soviet Union, *FT*, 12 Mar. 1990.
120. *Socialist Worker*, 22 Jul. 1989. A detailed account of the miners' strikes is given in T. Friedgut and L. Siegelbaum, 'Perestroika from Below', *NLR*, 181 (1990).
121. *Independent*, 7 Feb. 1990.
122. *FT*, 14 Feb. 1990.
123. See interview with Oleg Voronin, *Socialist Worker*, 2 Mar. 1990.
124. *Independent*, 8 Feb. 1990.
125. Harman, 'Stalinist States', p. 17.
126. *FT*, 27 Jan. 1990.
127. Ibid., 20 Nov. 1989.
128. B. Kagarlitsky, 'The Importance of Being Marxist', *NLR*, 178 (1989) pp. 32–3.
129. *FT*, 19 Feb. 1990.
130. *Independent*, 13 Apr. 1990.
131. *FT*, 19 Jan. 1990.
132. Quoted in Harman, 'The Storm Breaks', p. 81.
133. *Socialist Worker*, 2 Mar. 1990. See also B. Kagarlitsky, *Farewell Perestroika* (London, 1990). However, the Committee for a New Socialist Party's strategic conception of 'revolutionary reformism' is indicative of considerable confusion over whether the existing Russian state can be gradually modified or must be overthrown: see my review of Kagarlitsky's *Dialectic of Change*, 'A Third Road?', *Socialist Worker Review*, Feb. 1990.

CHAPTER 3   The Triumph of the West?

1. F. Fukuyama, 'The End of History?', *The National Interest*, Summer 1989, p. 3.

2. Chris Harman has analysed the economic causes, and traced the political course of the crisis of the 1970s and early 1980s in, respectively, *Explaining the Crisis* (London, 1984) and *The Fire Last Time* (London, 1988).
3. *FT*, 20 Sep. 1989.
4. One of the best elaborated versions of this theory is to be found in D. Harvey, *The Condition of Postmodernity* (Oxford, 1989). I have criticized the idea of a qualitatively new phase of capitalist development in *Against Postmodernism* (Cambridge, 1990), ch. 5. The concept of 'multinational capitalism' used in the last chapter does not refer to any such distinct phase, both because of the continued importance of the state despite the internationalization of capital, and because the tendency towards global integration in no sense represents the long-term stabilization of the world economy after the crises of the 1970s and early 1980s.
5. *FT*, 7 Sep. 1982.
6. Survey on the World Economy, *FT*, 26 Sep. 1989. 'World GNP' here excludes the USSR and most of Comecon.
7. *FT*, 31 May 1989.
8. Ibid., 13 Oct. 1989.
9. *Independent*, 24 Apr. 1990.
10. Survey on the World Economy, *FT*, 26 Sep. 1989.
11. *FT*, 22 Sep. 1986.
12. Ibid., 8 Sep. 1986.
13. Ibid., 27 Jul. 1987.
14. Ibid., 30 Jun. 1988.
15. Ibid., 22 Nov. 1989.
16. Ibid., 19 Feb. 1990.
17. Ibid., 1 Mar. 1990.
18. Ibid., 23 Apr. 1990.
19. See A. Callinicos, 'Imperialism, Capitalism and the State Today', *IS*, 2:35 (1987), pp. 88–94.
20. P. Kennedy, *The Rise and Fall of the Great Powers* (London, 1989), pp. xxii–xxiii.
21. Survey on the World Economy, *FT*, 26 Sep. 1989. For an interesting if overly conspiratorial history of the political integration of US and West European capitalism, see K. van der Pijl, *The Making of an Atlantic Ruling Class* (London, 1984).
22. Harman, *Explaining*, pp. 93–9.
23. F. Halliday, *The Making of the Second Cold War* (London, 1983).
24. Kennedy, *Rise and Fall*, chs 5 and 6.
25. Survey on the World Economy, *FT*, 26 Sep. 1989.
26. *FT*, 6 Oct. 1989.
27. Ibid., 30 Nov. 1989.
28. Ibid., 1 Dec. 1989.
29. Ibid., 5 Dec. 1989.

30. Ibid., 6 Dec. 1989.
31. *Independent*, 1 Mar. 1990.
32. N. Bobbio, 'The Upturned Utopia', *NLR*, 177 (1989), p. 39.
33. *FT*, 13 Dec. 1989.
34. *Independent*, 15 Dec. 1989.
35. *FT*, 14 Dec. 1989.
36. Ibid., 11 Jan. 1990.
37. Ibid., 30 Nov. 1989.
38. Ibid., 30 Jan. 1990.
39. Melbourne *Age*, 5 Apr. 1988.
40. A remark made during Frank's contribution to a panel on 'Where We Are in History', Socialist Scholars' Conference, New York, 8 Apr. 1990.
41. F. Halliday, *Cold War, Third World* (London, 1989), p. 70, and ch. 3 *passim*.
42. A. Cockburn, 'Backyard Stench', *New Statesman and Society*, 18 May 1990, p. 19. See also M. Gellhorn, 'The Invasion of Panama', *Granta*, 32 (1990).
43. F. Halliday, 'The Ends of the Cold War', *NLR*, 180 (1990), p. 9.
44. *FT*, 27 Mar. 1990.
45. Ibid., 24 Oct. 1988.
46. B. Kagarlitsky, 'The Importance of Being Marxist', *NLR*, 178 (1989), p. 35.
47. M. Kundera, 'A Kidnapped Western Culture Bows Out', *Granta*, 11 (1984), pp. 95, 97–102.
48. See, for example, Ian Thompson's letter in *Granta*, 13 (1984), pp. 267–8.
49. C. L. R. James, *Notes on Dialectics* (London, 1980), p. 136.
50. T. G. Ash, *The Uses of Adversity* (Cambridge, 1989), pp. 165–6.
51. J. Szücs, 'Three Historical Regions of Europe', in J. Keane (ed.), *Civil Society and the State* (London, 1988), esp. pp. 322–30. The cultural diversity of *Mitteleuropa* is brilliantly conveyed by Claudio Magris in *Danube* (London, 1989).
52. See C. Schorske, *Fin-de-Siècle Vienna* (New York, 1981).
53. Ash, *Uses*, p. 166.
54. E. J. Hobsbawm, *The Age of Empire 1875–1914* (London, 1987), p. 279.
55. M. Vajda, 'East-Central European Perspectives', in Keane (ed.), *Civil Society*, pp. 333–4.
56. Quoted in *Socialist Worker Review*, Dec. 1989.
57. W. Benjamin, *Illuminations* (London, 1970), p. 258.
58. See R. Augstein et al., *'Historikerstreit'* (Munich, 1987), the special issue of *New German Critique*, 44 (1988), and, for a refutation of the idea of a German *Sonderweg* (special path), D. Blackbourn and G. Eley, *The Peculiarities of German History* (Oxford, 1984). Detlev Peukert draws on the findings of *Alltagsgeschichte*, the history of everyday life

under Hitler, to present a convincing interpretation of Nazism as a consequence of the contradictions of modernity, though for some reason he believes this view to be inconsistent with the Marxist theory of fascism: see *Inside Nazi Germany* (Harmondsworth, 1989).

59. G. Barraclough, *European Unity in Theory and Practice* (Oxford, 1963), p. 41.
60. J. Herrin, *The Formation of Christendom* (Oxford, 1987), p. 8.
61. D. Hay, *Europe: the Emergence of an Idea* (Edinburgh, 1957), esp. chs 6 and 7.
62. E. W. Said, *Orientalism* (Harmondsworth, 1985).
63. Ibid., pp. 206–7.
64. P. Alexander, *Race, Resistance, and Revolution* (London, 1987).
65. A. Barnett, H. M. Enzensberger, and B. Kagarlitsky, 'Back in the USSR', *New Statesman and Society*, 10 Nov. 1989, p. 26.
66. Barraclough, *European Unity*, e.g., pp. 7–21.
67. N. Ascherson, 'Old Conflicts in the New Europe', *Independent on Sunday* Sunday Review, 18 Feb. 1990, p. 5.
68. J. Hough, *Russia and the West*, 2nd edn (New York, 1990), pp. 179–80, 205–6. According to Oleg Voronin, eye-witness accounts suggest that the anti-Armenian pogroms used to justify the military occupation of Baku in January 1990 were incited by 'agents of the local party apparatus and the KGB': interview in *Socialist Worker*, 2 Mar. 1990.
69. Kennedy, *Rise and Fall*, pp. 609–10.
70. 'Report on Economic and Monetary Union in the European Community', extracts in *FT*, 18 Apr. 1989 (italics in original).
71. P. Hirst, 'Endism', *London Review of Books*, 23 Nov. 1989, p. 14.
72. J. Grahl and P. Teague, 'The Cost of Neo-Liberal Europe', *NLR*, 174 (1989), p. 35.
73. 'Mitterrand the Monetarist', editorial in *FT*, 20 Apr. 1990.
74. *FT*, 7 Feb. 1990. The erosion of Swedish corporatism had in fact been under way for some time: see S. Lash and J. Urry, *The End of Organized Capitalism* (Cambridge, 1987).

CHAPTER 4   Beyond the Market

1. See, for example, I. Forbes (ed.), *Market Socialism: Whose Choice?* (London, 1986).
2. Speech at Socialist Movement Conference on Gorbachev and the Left, Oxford, 3 June 1989.
3. For example, B. Kagarlitsky, 'The Market instead of Democracy?', *IS*, 2:45 (1989).
4. T. G. Ash, *We the People* (Cambridge, 1990), p. 151.
5. L. von Mises, 'Economic Calculation in the Socialist Commonwealth',

in F. A. von Hayek (ed.), *Collectivist Economic Planning* (London, 1935), pp. 104, 106. See also L. Robbins, *The Great Depression* (London, 1934), pp. 145–56.

6. O. Lange and F. M. Taylor, *On the Economic Theory of Socialism* (New York, 1964). Some of the criticisms of this solution made by Maurice Dobb in *On Economic Theory and Socialism* (London, 1955) are, however, valid, even though they are deployed in defence of the Stalinist command economy.

7. A. Nove, *The Economics of Feasible Socialism* (London, 1983), pp. 59, 33.

8. C. Harman, 'The Myth of Market Socialism', *IS*, 2:42 (1989), and E. Mandel, 'In Defence of Socialist Planning', *NLR*, 159 (1986). See also M. Haynes, 'Nightmares of the Market', *IS*, 2:41 (1988), which discusses the two main claimed successes of market socialism, Yugoslavia and Hungary.

9. T. Cliff, *Russia: a Marxist Analysis*, 3rd edn (London, 1970), ch. 12, and C. Harman, 'Poland: Crisis of State Capitalism', *IS*, 93 and 94 (1976–7).

10. Nove, *Economics*, p. 201.

11. Harman, 'Myth', p. 18.

12. R. Nozick, *Anarchy, State and Utopia* (Oxford, 1974). For Marxist criticisms of Nozick, see esp. G. A. Cohen, 'Nozick on Appropriation', *NLR*, 150 (1985).

13. D. Miller, *Market, State, and Community* (Oxford, 1989), pp. 128, 174, 189. See, more generally, ibid., Part II. Roberto Unger's 'programme of empowered democracy' involves rather similar economic arrangements to Miller's market socialism and is liable to the same objections: see *False Necessity* (Cambridge, 1987). Unger's theory of history is criticized in P. Anderson, 'Roberto Unger and the Politics of Empowerment', *NLR*, 173 (1989).

14. *FT*, 3 Apr. 1985. See also A. Sen, *Poverty and Famines* (Oxford, 1982).

15. *FT*, 20 Apr. 1990.

16. K. Marx, *Capital*, II (Moscow, 1956), p. 499.

17. See, for example, N. Harris, *Of Bread and Guns* (Harmondsworth, 1983), S. Lash and J. Urry, *The End of Organized Capitalism* (Cambridge, 1987), and, for some qualifications, A. Callinicos, *Against Postmodernism* (Cambridge, 1990), ch. 5.

18. For example, K. Marx, 'Results of the Immediate Process of Production', Appendix to *Capital*, I (Harmondsworth, 1976), pp. 1025–34, and *Grundrisse* (Harmondsworth, 1973), pp. 283–4; but see, on the latter passage, E. M. Wood, 'Rational Choice Marxism', *NLR*, 177 (1989), pp. 56–8.

19. *Independent*, 9 Jan. 1989.

20. G. Lipovetsky, *L'Ère du vide* (Paris, 1983).

21. See esp. K. Marx, *Capital*, III (Moscow, 1971), pp. 264–5.

22. See, for example, F. Pearce, *Turning Up the Heat* (London, 1989), esp. ch. 13. I am grateful to Ian Taylor for drawing this book to my attention.
23. S. Hecht and A. Cockburn, *The Fate of the Forest* (London, 1989).
24. A. Heller, 'On Formal Democracy', in J. Keane (ed.), *Civil Society and the State* (London, 1988), pp. 130, 131, 133.
25. T. G. Ash, *We the People*, p. 147.
26. Z. A. Pelczynski, 'Solidarity and "the Rebirth of Civil Society" in Poland, 1976–81', in Keane (ed.), *Civil Society*, p. 363.
27. N. Bobbio, 'Gramsci and the Conception of Civil Society', in id., *Which Socialism?* (Cambridge, 1986), and in Keane (ed.), *Civil Society*. For a critical discussion of the distinction between the state and civil society, see E. M. Wood, 'The Uses and Abuses of "Civil Society"', in R. Miliband and L. Panitch (eds), *Socialist Register 1990* (London, 1990).
28. Pelczynski, 'Solidarity', pp. 367–8.
29. Keane, editor's introduction to *Civil Society*, pp. 19–20.
30. Ash, *We the People*, pp. 148–9.
31. Heller, 'Formal Democracy', p. 131.
32. Bobbio, *Which Socialism?*, p. 43.
33. Ibid., pp. 43, 100–1.
34. *Independent*, 7 May 1990.
35. Claims by Antonio Negri to the effect that 'democracy is a played out form with a purely obscurantist function, a blanket term for a system of power completely dominated by the collective forces of capital' therefore have nothing to do with the classical Marxist tradition: 'Is There a Marxist Doctrine of the State? A Reply', in Bobbio, *Which Socialism?*, p. 125. It is hardly surprising that, faced with revolutionary opponents such as Negri, Bobbio's writings had such an impact on the Italian left.
36. It would not be appropriate here to discuss the mechanisms through which specific state-forms are brought to operate in the interests of capital (or the theoretical problems involved in analysing these mechanisms). B. Jessop, *The Capitalist State* (Oxford, 1982), is a useful survey.
37. See P. Anderson, 'The Affinities of Norberto Bobbio', *NLR*, 170 (1988).
38. See, for example, Bobbio's very scrappy discussion of three variants of direct democracy in *Which Socialism?*, pp. 79–84.
39. It is one of the merits of David Held's *Models of Democracy* (Cambridge, 1987) that it recognizes the first, though not the second, of these aspects of historical forms of democracy.
40. See E. M. Wood, *Peasant-Citizen and Slave* (London, 1988), and my review, 'The Foundations of Athenian Democracy', *IS*, 2:40 (1988).
41. L. D. Trotsky, *1905* (Harmondsworth, 1973), p. 266.
42. Id., *The Spanish Revolution (1931–39)* (New York, 1973), p. 85. See

also *Leon Trotsky on China* (New York, 1976), pp. 319–20.
43. *LCW*, XXX, p. 264.
44. D. Gluckstein, *The Western Soviets* (London, 1985), R. Fraser, *Blood of Spain* (Harmondsworth, 1981), C. Harman, *Class Struggles in Eastern Europe, 1945–83* (London, 1983), ch. 7, C. Barker (ed.), *Revolutionary Rehearsals* (London, 1987), A. Bayat, *Workers and Revolution in Iran* (London, 1987), and C. Barker, *Festival of the Oppressed* (London, 1986). I discuss the theory and practice of soviet democracy in 'Soviet Power', *IS*, 103 (1977).
45. A. Gramsci, *Selections from Political Writings 1910–1920* (London, 1977), p. 65.
46. *LCW*, XXV, p. 466.
47. Bobbio, *Which Socialism?*, p. 84.
48. The tacit reliance of capitalist production on the know-how and co-operation of the workforce it exploits and alienates is one of the main themes of Cornelius Castoriadis's thought in its Marxist phase: see *Social and Political Writings* (2 vols, Minneapolis, 1988).
49. See A. Callinicos and C. Harman, *The Changing Working Class* (London, 1987), L. German, *Sex, Class and Socialism* (London, 1989), and Callinicos, *Against Postmodernism*, pp. 121–7.
50. T. Wolforth, 'Transition to the Transition', *NLR*, 130 (1981), p. 79.
51. Held, *Models*, p. 131 n. 8.
52. See J. Reed, 'Soviets in Action', *IS*, 67 (1974), p. 20, and D. Mandel, *The Petrograd Workers and the Seizure of Power* (Basingstoke, 1984), pp. 351–7.
53. *MECW*, XX, pp. 332–4.
54. Held, *Models*, pp. 137–8.
55. L. D. Trotsky, *The Revolution Betrayed* (New York, 1972), pp. 266–7. Critics of Trotsky often contrast his commitment to multi-party soviets in 1937 with the defence of large-scale coercion in works of the Civil War such as *Terrorism and Communism* (London, 1975), first published in 1920. These criticisms do not sufficiently take into account either the acute crisis of the immediate post-Revolutionary years – on which see now T. Cliff, *Trotsky: the Sword of the Revolution 1917–23* (London, 1990) – or the extent to which he subsequently moved away from the identification of soviet power with one-party rule made by the Bolsheviks during those years. Trotsky's evolving views of the relationship between party and class are discussed in some illuminating essays collected in N. Geras, *Literature of Revolution* (London, 1986).
56. Trotsky, *Revolution Betrayed*, p. 266.
57. See O. H. Radkey, *The Elections to the Russian Constituent Assembly of 1917* (Cambridge, Mass., 1950). Compare Lenin's interesting discussion in 'The Constituent Assembly Elections and the Dictatorship of the Proletariat', in *LCW*, XXX.
58. M. Liebman, *Leninism under Lenin* (London, 1975), p. 237.

59. Ibid., p. 236.
60. Raymond Williams discusses ways of democratizing the mass media in *Communications* (Harmondsworth, 1968), ch. 5.
61. *MECW*, XXIV, p. 94.
62. Ibid., XXXIX, pp. 62, 65.
63. Ibid., XXIV, p. 87.
64. L. D. Trotsky, *Writings (1932)* (New York, 1973), pp. 273–4. Trotsky goes on to attack Stalin's 'administrative suppression of the NEP', on the grounds that '[e]conomic accounting is unthinkable without market relations', and to argue for 'a planned retreat' involving the restoration of market mechanisms. *'Il faut reculer pour mieux sauter*: Let us retreat in order the better to advance.' (Ibid., pp. 276, 279.) These arguments did not simply represent Trotsky's reaction to the First Five-Year Plan; he had developed the same theme, of the interdependence of market and plan, in the early 1920s: see Cliff, *Trotsky*, pp. 239–44.
65. On this general conception of the transition period, see P. Binns and D. Hallas, 'The Soviet Union – State Capitalist or Socialist?', *IS*, 91 (1976), and E. Balibar, *On the Dictatorship of the Proletariat* (London, 1977).
66. Nove, *Economics*, pp. 15–17.
67. F. Pearce, 'In Defence of Population Growth', *New Scientist*, 9 Aug. 1984, p. 15.
68. Cited in Pearce, *Turning Up the Heat*, pp. 180–2.
69. Marx, 'Results', p. 1068.
70. See, for example, D. Wiggins, 'The Claims of Need', in T. Honderich (ed.), *Morality and Objectivity* (London, 1985).
71. N. Geras, 'The Controversy about Marx and Justice', *NLR*, 150 (1985), p. 82. Geras adverts to the distinction between needs and wants on p. 83.
72. Ibid., pp. 82–3.
73. Lange and Taylor, *Economic Theory*, pp. 139–41. Mandel develops this argument at greater length: 'Defence', pp. 14–21.
74. See, for example, D. Elson, 'Market Socialism or Socialization of the Market?', *NLR*, 172 (1988), and P. Devine, *Democracy and Economic Planning* (Cambridge, 1988).
75. *MECW*, XXIV, p. 87.
76. K. Marx, *Theories of Surplus-Value*, I (Moscow, 1963), p. 401.
77. Id., *Grundrisse*, p. 611.
78. Id., *Capital*, III, p. 820.
79. *MECW*, V, p. 47.
80. A. Rattansi, *Marx and the Division of Labour* (London, 1982).
81. G. A. Cohen, 'Reconsidering Historical Materialism', in A. Callinicos (ed.), *Marxist Theory* (Oxford, 1989), pp. 159–61. Cohen's further doubt whether creative activity exhausts human fulfilment, and Terry Eagleton's related doubt whether the '"all-round" development' of

human powers is in any case an unqualified good – see *The Ideology of the Aesthetic* (Oxford, 1990), ch. 8 – do not seriously weaken Marx's case for communism so long as it is accepted that creative activity is an essential component of self-realization.

82. *MECW*, V, p. 47.
83. See Callinicos and Harman, *Changing Working Class*, ch. 1.
84. J. Elster, *Making Sense of Marx* (Cambridge, 1985), p. 526.
85. *MECW*, VI, p. 506.
86. Ibid., IV, p. 131.
87. Elster, *Making Sense*, p. 526.
88. *MECW*, XXIV, pp. 86–7.
89. P. Anderson, 'Modernity and Revolution', in C. Nelson and L. Grossberg, *Marxism and the Interpretation of Culture* (Basingstoke, 1988), p. 336. Anderson talks here of socialism, but describes a state of affairs likely only to be stably established with the advent of communism.
90. K. Marx, *A Contribution to the Critique of Political Economy* (London, 1971), pp. 21–2. Compare Kautsky's interesting, if somewhat Darwinian, comments on individual competition under socialism in *The Agrarian Question* (2 vols, London, 1988), II, p. 208.
91. L. D. Trotsky, *Literature and Revolution* (Ann Arbor, Michigan, 1971), pp. 230–1.
92. For a recent discussion of pluralism which never gets much beyond elegant fence-sitting, see G. MacLennan, *Marxism, Pluralism and Beyond* (Cambridge, 1989).
93. *LCW*, XXV, p. 461.
94. *MECW*, VI, p. 505.
95. Ibid., XXIV, p. 71.
96. *LCW*, XXV, p. 469.
97. See, on nationality, A. Callinicos, *Making History* (Cambridge, 1987), chs 4 and 5, and, on gender, L. German, *Sex, Class and Socialism*.
98. See A. Callinicos, 'Marxism and Politics', in A. Leftwich (ed.), *What is Politics?* (Oxford, 1984). Andrew Levine's argument in *The End of the State* (London, 1987) that '[t]he end of the state yields a social order where individuals devote their lives to public deliberation and debate and even collective choice' (pp. 172–3) accords fully with the theme of this section: unfortunately, the book is gravely weakened by Levine's acceptance, under the influence of John Roemer, of the idea that socialism involves forms of exploitation (pp. 108–19).
99. N. Geras, 'Seven Types of Obloquy', in Miliband and Panitch (eds), *Socialist Register 1990*.
100. Marx, *Grundrisse*, p. 488.

Conclusion

1. *MECW*, VI, p. 487.

INDEX